# Critics Are Raving About
# REEL LEADERSHIP
## DISCOVERING THE HIDDEN
## LEADERSHIP LESSONS IN MOVIES

———

I don't think I'll ever watch a movie the same way again. In addition to viewing for entertainment value, I'll be asking myself what I can learn, how I would handle the situations in the story, and how I can be a better leader in my own reality.
— **Nathan Magnuson, Executive Consultant and CEO, Leadership-in-a-Box**

*Reel Leadership* looks at the intersection of leadership and movies through examples and practical steps to start viewing movies through the lens of leadership.
— **Marty Himmel, watched a movie a day for 366 days**

"If you like movies, you're going to love it. If you're a leader, you're going to love it. If you're a leader who also loves movies this book will reel you in. Joe Lalonde's *Reel Leadership* is a deep dive into leadership "Easter eggs" embedded in the films we all love.

— **Chester Goad, Actor, Film Creator, Stand-Up Comic, ChesterG.com, and Author of *Purple People Leader***

"One of the unfortunate casualties of today's entrepreneur hustle culture is good entertainment. If you're working so hard that you miss great storytelling, you're robbing yourself (and your team) of great lessons you can learn no other way. In his fantastic book *Reel Leadership*, Joseph Lalonde gives us a clear and fun guide to learning leadership from the movies. You don't need to feel guilty about watching TV and movies—they can be a great source of wisdom when you follow the principles in this amazing book!

— **Kent Sanders, College Professor, Author of *The Artist's Suitcase***

# REEL LEADERSHIP

# REEL LEADERSHIP

## DISCOVERING THE HIDDEN LEADERSHIP LESSONS IN MOVIES

JOSEPH LALONDE

NEW DEGREE PRESS

COPYRIGHT © 2021 JOSEPH LALONDE

REEL LEADERSHIP

*Discovering the Hidden Leadership Lessons in Movies*

ISBN     978-1-63730-700-7-*Paperback*

           978-1-63730-791-5-*Kindle Ebook*

           979-8-88504-015-0-*Ebook*

*For Pamela, my wife,*

*You've been a gem as I've pursued this journey of personal development, becoming a better leader, and doing this writing thing. Without you, this would be nothing.*

*For Mr. Gibner,*

*I will never forget how you helped instill the love of writing in me through your English class. Your words and inspiration have stuck with me through the years.*

*For the movie producers,*

*Your visionary films have filled my life with joy. I hope this book will inspire and encourage others to enjoy your works.*

*For the tired and worn-out leader,*

*You can enjoy yourself. Go watch a movie. Find a way to unwind.*

*For my father,*

*I wish you were here to see this published. You were always so proud of me.*

# CONTENTS

---

# INTRODUCTION

———

*"It takes a great deal of bravery to stand up to your enemies, but a great deal more to stand up to your friends."*

*"There is a difference between knowing the path and walking the path."*

*"If you want to know what a man's like, take a good look at how he treats his inferiors, not his equals."*

*"The world ain't all sunshine and rainbows. It is a very mean and nasty place, and it will beat you to your knees and keep you there permanently if you let it. You, me, or nobody is gonna hit as hard as life. But it ain't how hard you get hit; it's about how hard you get hit and keep moving forward."*

*"I don't want to be a product of my environment. I want my environment to be a product of me."*

*"You shouldn't want them all to think the same. It is their different points of view that make the team strong. A good leader understands this. A good brother accepts it."*

Growing up, I remember going to the movies and having such a great time. They provided stories of people I would never meet, in places I would never see. These people were in situations that I never would have to face myself and, there on the big screen, these people were fighting, challenging, and struggling for something more, something better than what they had.

These great movies included *Teenage Mutant Ninja Turtles, Uncle Buck, Jurassic Park, Godzilla, Batman Returns, Twister,* and so many others. When these movies released every Friday, they were an escape—a beautiful picture of what people could overcome, as well as what they could enjoy. Movies were the escape I needed. You may have needed this escape too. It was the thing to do on a Friday or Saturday night if you wanted to leave the world you're in and just veg out for an hour and a half to two hours.

These movies were such an inspiration to me. Scenes and quotes in these movies struck me with awe and wonder, and I enjoyed it so much. As I got older, something changed, and I began watching movies less often. There was a reason for it. I wanted to become successful. I wanted to become secure. I wanted my life to count for something, and I believed, incorrectly, that I couldn't do this if I watched movies.

Why did this change, this shift, happen?

I began to read books, listen to podcasts, and listen to successful speakers. They always mentioned the statistics of successful people and what they did or didn't do. What were these things successful people didn't do? They didn't listen to music, watch television shows, or—*gasp!*—go to the movies. Thomas Corley, the author of *Rich Habits: The Daily Success Habits of Wealthy Individuals*, studied the habits of the rich and successful. His findings discovered that 67 percent of rich and successful people only watch TV for one hour or less per day.

They included movies in all the things they didn't do. Yes, that's right. Successful people supposedly didn't watch movies. I bought into that. I bought into this theory that successful people don't go to movies; they don't allow themselves to enjoy movies or entertainment.

But something changed in me as I continued my journey: I discovered movies and entertainment are a great teaching tool. We can find leadership lessons, we can find moral lessons, we can even find life lessons in movies. That's what this book is all about: the lessons we can find in movies. It's not the easiest path to take. But it's a really, really cool path when you think about it. When you're able to sit down, grab your movie theater popcorn, and find leadership lessons in the movies that you already enjoy.

Who wouldn't want to do something like that?

I know I find a lot of enjoyment in watching a great movie, and I bet you do too, even if you don't want to admit to watching a movie here or there. You may struggle with the idea that you can go watch a movie and walk away with a new leadership idea or principle. You may tell yourself, *I can't do that. That's not right. That's not how people become successful. They don't sit down for two hours, watch a movie, and learn from it.*

I'm ready to flip this idea on its head.

In fact, the same people who taught me that entertainment isn't for successful people also taught me the concept of *reel leadership*—the term I've coined for looking at movies while intending to pull out leadership lessons. That's weird, huh? Weird as it may be, it's the truth. When podcasters and authors talk about the stories from which they learn and how stories are so important for drawing people into messages and allowing them to process what's being said, my idea of movies changed again.

One of the key elements for this change was when these leadership experts were talking about fables and how great they were. They said fables could teach people about leadership and moral lessons. That made me stop, think, and wonder why then do we talk so negatively about movies. Fables are legendary stories intended to enforce a useful truth. Movies are just long stories with visuals and audio. They're a perfect mix of everything that a story should be, and apparently, we're not looking at them in the right way.

We're telling people to stay away from movies. We're telling people not to watch a movie. They're a waste of time. Mindless entertainment, if you will. Don't involve yourself in the entertainment industry because it's just going to rot your brain out. Movies will not teach you, or you will learn nothing. Movies will not help you become a better person or a more successful person or even a leader.

These thoughts and ideas are not going to fly in this book.

Movies are not a waste of time if you're intentional about watching the movie you're viewing. What does being intentional about watching the movie mean? It means you watch with eyes and ears trained to see and hear the hidden messages shared through the movie. It's not purely a piece of entertainment. There are premises the producers may have slid into the movie, even if they do not realize this. In his book *The Moral Premise*, author and screenwriter Stanley Williams shares with aspiring film writers what he thinks makes a film successful. Having a teaching premise is one of the main reasons. It's also a reason *you* can learn from the movies.

Every movie has a lesson that the movie producer or director wants to teach the movie watcher. We're going to look at this idea of the moral premise because it's an excellent theory when you watch a movie. Know that people have a reason for the things they create—even for the entertainment they create. We can see things in movies. We can find these lessons if we actually look at the things we're consuming.

So sit back; get ready. We're going to dive into some reel leadership.

We're going to delve into the leadership lessons we can find in movies. We're going to discover that movies are a fantastic way to learn, grow, and engross yourself in leadership.

Before we go further, let's rewind for a minute. Let's head back to the beginning of this chapter. I want to expose you to something you may not have realized I did.

I opened this introduction with six different quotes. Each of these quotes spoke to me. They made me think about leadership and how to lead well. I hope they made you think about leadership too.

Think about the six quotes above. How do they make you think about leadership? Do they give you an idea to pursue in treating your employees? Do they make you think about integrity in leadership? Do they make you think about the challenge of challenging other leaders in your organization? Do they make you think of the failures you have faced in business and how you had to get up again and again? Maybe they make you think of the culture of your organization? About how you have the power to help shape the environment around you? Or did the quotes help you think about diversity in the workplace?

Who do you think said these words? Is it the late, great Zig Ziglar? Maybe it is Tony Robbins? Could it be an obscure but wise business leader?

If you thought of those influential leaders, you would be wrong. None of these quotes came from a business professional. Instead, these quotes are from the movies. These were words spoken by fictional characters in a film.

- The first quote is from Professor Dumbledore in *Harry Potter and the Sorcerer's Stone.*
- The second quote is from Morpheus in *The Matrix.*

- The third quote is from Sirius Black in *Harry Potter and the Goblet of Fire.*
- The fourth quote is from the boxer Rocky Balboa in *Rocky.*
- The fifth quote is from Frank Costello in *The Departed.*
- The last quote is from Master Splinter as he talked to Leonardo in *Teenage Mutant Ninja Turtles: Out of The Shadows.*

The quote from Frank Costello in *The Departed* really spoke to me—it should be a motto of every leader. Remember what Frank said? He said, "I don't want to be a product of my environment. I want my environment to be a product of me." Can we encapsulate what leadership is any better than this? This flows right in line with John Maxwell's signature line, "Leadership is influence. Nothing more, nothing less." When we are no longer a product of our environment and we are, instead, making the environment a product of you or me, we're leading.

Crazy, huh?

That's the power of movies. They don't have to bore you or put you to sleep like so many leadership seminars. They don't have to be dull.

Movies are entertainment, sure. But movies can be so much more. They are a window into a world you've never experienced before. They open the possibility for you to connect with characters you would never come across in real life. Movies can even give you greater empathy for the people you lead.

In *Life Itself*, a documentary about the life and career of film critic Robert Ebert, we see and hear Robert Ebert say, "The purpose of civilization and growth is to be able to reach out and empathize a little bit with other people. And for me, the movies are like a machine that generates empathy. It lets you understand a little more about different hopes, aspirations, dreams, and fears."

It's my hope that you will discover the same ideas within this book. Your eyes will open to the possibility of a *whole new world* (Aladdin anyone?), as I opened my eyes to the world of *reel leadership.*

I'm so glad I discovered this; however, I'm disappointed that it took me so long to figure it out. Once I did, I began to enjoy the things I used to enjoy. I'm growing and I'm learning, and things are looking up.

So, as we begin this journey, I want to invite you in; I want to invite you to become a "reel leader." It's going to be fun, it's going to take some time, it's going to be a challenge, but throughout this book, you're going to see something. You're going to see how to find leadership principles in movies.

It's a journey we can take together. We can explore the leadership thoughts hidden within the movies we all enjoy. I love this journey. I am hopeful you will too.

Now, ladies and gentlemen, it is time to dive into *Reel Leadership* and discover the leadership lessons in the movies all around us. This book will be a tool to show you the lessons you can discover. It will help you see the leadership lessons displayed on the big screen. More than that, *Reel Leadership* will help you apply these lessons to the way you lead in your organization and in your life.

Like any good movie, though, I hope you don't keep the ideas in *Reel Leadership* to yourself. When you discover a great movie, you don't keep it to yourself; you go out and talk to your friends and family about it. You share the thrills, chills, and excitement you experienced. Do that with this book. As you read, think about who could benefit from *Reel Leadership*. Then share it with that person. You will help spread the message behind the book, but more importantly, you will help others discover leadership from the movies.

# ACT 1

# SCENE 1:

# THE HISTORY OF FILM

———

*"Ever wonder why history repeats itself?"*
— SENATOR DIANNE FEINSTEIN, *THE REPORT*

This may shock you to discover, but movies have actually been around a lot longer than you may think. When I started writing this book, I thought movies were a fairly recent invention—maybe fifty or seventy-five years old. I was wrong.

Movie production began in approximately 1888. Discovering that movies, even short movies, have been around for over 130 years blows my mind. It's hard to believe movies have been around that long.

The world of movies is such an ingrained part of our lives these days. Multiple movies release each week, or that has been the normal release schedule pre-COVID. Think about this: In the early days of film, maybe one **short** movie released every **three** years. Now, we are seeing multiple movies released a week. That's quite the change!

Let me share with you some of the first movies recorded and shared with the world.

The first recorded movie I found in my research was filmed in 1888. It was titled *Roundhay Garden Scene*. Produced by Lewis Le Prince and filmed in the United Kingdom, the moving picture ran a staggering 2.11 seconds. *Roundhay Garden Scene* was definitely not the longest movie ever. However, the short picture was something new and different.

The first longer form movie was titled *Pantomimes Lumineuses*. It was produced and directed by Charles Emile Reynad in France. He released the film in October 1892. An interesting fact about *Pantomimes Lumineuses* is that it was not a live-action film. *Pantomimes Lumineuses* was the first animated film ever created. It was also the longest film of the time.

More than this, *Pantomimes Lumineuses* holds another distinction. It is a collection of different short films. *Pantomimes Lumineuses* is a collection of three films put into one: *Le Clown et ses chiens*, *Pauvre Pierrot*, and *Un bon bok*. The total running time for this collection of animated movies was forty-five minutes. This was much longer than *Roundhay Garden Scene* and began to change the length of movies.

*Le Clown et ses chiens* told the story of a circus clown. The clown entered the circus ring and greeted the audience. He then performed tricks by making three dogs jump through hoops, walk on a ball, and jump over a wand.

*Pauvre Pierrot* told the story of Pierrot. As a man meets his love, Pierrot knocks on Columbina's door and the couple takes cover. Pierrot begins a serenade, but the man interrupts Pierrot's performance. It lasted approximately fifteen minutes.

*Un bon bok* tells the story of a wanderer going into a countryside cabaret. He asks a waitress for a beer. The wanderer swoons over the waitress, and he tries to enchant the young woman.

Looking at the runtime of the ten oldest movies, it may shock you to discover they were extremely short. Most of the films were under a minute. Five of the ten oldest movies had a runtime of under forty seconds!

On the other hand, the *Corbett-Fitzsimmons Fight*, a documentary filming of a boxing match between James J. Corbett and Bob Fitzsimmons, ran over one hundred minutes. It took place in Carson City, Nevada, on St. Patrick's Day 1897, and was the first feature-length film ever produced. It was the longest film of the time.

It can be hard for us to understand or comprehend a one-hundred-minute movie being the longest film made. When we look at movies in the modern era, film runtimes are much longer. Movies today often run 120 minutes or more—we've even seen movies occasionally run into the three- or four-hour length.

When films first came out, you couldn't film a really long movie. The technology just didn't exist. These films were black and white. They were silent. They didn't have the engaging qualities that films of today have. This was a different era of film. It was an era where films were being birthed for the first time. People loved the quirky films. Today, there would be a much different reaction.

## THE RISE OF THE MOVIE STAR

Unlike movies today, many of the early films (films in the 1890s–1900s) did not name their actors. Movies didn't have the big-name stars. There was no Dwayne "The Rock" Johnson, Margot Robbie, Bruce Willis, Gal Gadot, Chris Evans, Blake Lively, Jason Momoa, or Emma Stone. They did this for a specific reason. Why didn't the studios want to name actors? The movie studios didn't want to create stars and the rising salaries (we all know higher salaries eat into organizational budgets). These increase costs all around.

This changed in 1912 and 1913. One of the earliest stars was Charlie Chaplin. He started out making $130 a week, but within a year or two, he was making $10,000 a week or $500,000 a year. That was an enormous increase in wages. He went from making nothing to making half a million dollars. Other former stars of that era were Mary Pickford, Douglas Fairbanks, Jr., Fatty Arbuckle, and the Keystone Cops. Hollywood changed a lot in a few short years.

It's hard to understand but early films did not have big name stars. This was done to keep costs under control. However, once film stars began to rise, movies became more popular than ever.

Between those early days and the 1920s, Hollywood began courting stars and relying on stars to sell their movies. Directors had to find stars and high-profile actors to raise awareness of their upcoming movies. People wanted to see named stars. One of the nice things about it was these stars benefited from their exposure and movies. Wages rose, their profiles rose, and Hollywood began producing movies people really wanted to see. No longer were the actors in movies unknowns. Because of the increase in financing for films, everything in them improved.

We then run into the post-World War II era of movies. Once movies integrated sound in the post WWII era, attendance grew steadily. With the ability to add sound to movies, the studios quickly discovered people didn't want to see strictly moving pictures. Audiences wanted moving pictures that had sound and could bring them into the action that was happening.

Were there other innovations that happened?

Of course!

When you think of 3D movies, you probably think of James Cameron and his film, *Avatar*. James Cameron's film introduced film goers to a 3D world that blew us out of the water. The 3D effects in the film made moviegoers lose their minds and long for a sequel. But James Cameron wasn't the first to employ 3D technologies. Early 3D films include *The Power of Love* (1920), *House of Wax* (1952–55), and *Flesh for Frankenstein* (1973).

They also tried AromaRama, the first effective odor-distributing system for theaters. This technology was revolutionary. It could release scents you could quickly recognize and other scents that were familiar but not quite recognizable. The really interesting aspect of this is that they could clear the scent and introduce another at ninety-second intervals.

The drive-in theater was also another innovation in film. Instead of going into a building to watch a movie, you would drive your car to a field. As you entered the field, multiple other vehicles were around you. They were all there, waiting for darkness to fall and the screen to light up. The theater then projected the motion picture on a giant white screen in front of the vehicles.

To hear the audio, there were a couple of options. One of the speaker options was the Eprad drive-in movie theater window speaker you could place outside of your car window. More recently, they upgraded audio systems to allow you to use your car radio to tune into a local station and hear the movie's audio. The drive-in movie experience was, and is, really cool.

Unfortunately, drive-ins are almost a thing of the past. At the height of the drive-in theater craze, there were over 4,000 drive-in theaters in the United States. In 2020, only 321 drive-in theaters remained.

I've been able to experience the drive-in theater experience multiple times, as one of those 321 theaters is within driving distance of my home. Drive-in theaters are a novel experience that brings us back to a different time. Everyone should experience the drive-in at least once, if for nothing more than the novelty of the experience.

As technology continued to increase, something else changed in the movie industry. Instead of having to go to the theater to watch a big blockbuster movie, you could watch that big blockbuster movie in your home through the power of Betamax or VHS tapes. These tapes released to the public after the theatrical release. The great thing was you could now watch the biggest movies of the year on your home TV. This started happening in the mid-1980s. Betamax and VHS changed the landscape of the world of movies.

Hollywood originally hated this technology. They hated the fact that a person could watch the films in the privacy of their own homes. They thought it would undermine revenue they received from the movie theaters. Revenues did decrease for a short time, and this was one of the big frustrations for studios and theaters. However, the introduction of VHS technology wasn't completely a negative thing for Hollywood. Hollywood studios discovered this new technology actually diversified their revenue streams.

This was a bonus for studios and the movie viewer.

Watching a movie in the comfort of your home is nice, but there's something about going to the theaters, something about sitting in those comfy seats, something about the movie popcorn and a fountain pop. It's not the same watching a movie in your home. Sometimes you just have to experience movies in the theater, like the 2021 blockbuster movie *Godzilla vs. Kong.*

We really saw this in the 1990s. One of the biggest blockbusters of the '90s was the movie *Jurassic Park*. Steven Spielberg's film about scientists bringing dinosaurs to life in a theme park blew the minds of moviegoers. The technology Spielberg used to create these virtual dinosaurs was stunning. Surprisingly, thirty years later, they're still creating sequels to the original *Jurassic Park*, like *The Lost World: Jurassic Park* (1997), *Jurassic Park III* (2001), *Jurassic World* (2015), and *Jurassic World: Fallen Kingdom* (2018). Another sequel is in the works: *Jurassic World: Dominion*.

I believe this was the start of the new age of movies where it was about technology and making things look as jaw-droppingly real as possible. It wasn't necessarily about the story anymore. It was about how good they could make it look. Let me tell you: Movie studios can make things look really good.

For a while, these technological advances sufficed. Then, movies started suffering when producers tried to make the prettiest films and, in doing so, they neglected the storylines. Stunning visuals do not make a movie. Film production can't carry a movie. Technology can't carry the entire film; there has to be something more to it. There has to be a good story; there has to be a meaningful tale.

I believe there has to be a lesson in the movie. Movies are more than just moving pictures—they're moving stories. Movies are telling us something. They are bringing us into an environment that we can't enter by any other means.

The history of movies is very fascinating when you study it. The progression of movies moves rather quickly once it gets going.

To recap, we start out with short black-and-white films, no sound, no fancy visuals. We go to longer feature-length films of one hundred or more minutes. Next, we move into the era of the movie star and people gaining notoriety. This is the era of the Charlie Chaplin's of the movie world. Then, we move into technological advances such as trying 3D technology or AromaRama. And then, we move into this technologically advanced era of CGI, robotics, and making everything look as real as possible.

That's the magic of movies.

Because of the technological advances, we now see things that look as real as if we were looking out our picture window. If that isn't something special, I don't know what is. I'm looking forward to seeing what the future holds for movies and film production.

However, until more advances come, I'm still looking at the lessons that movies can teach.

## DISCUSSION QUESTIONS:

1. What surprised you the most about the history of film?
2. The film industry has changed over time. Our businesses and organizations do as well. What change are you fearful of? What possibilities could this change bring?
3. Look at the history of your organization. Does its trajectory look similar to the history of film? Where is it the same? Where is it different?
4. How can the history of film help you understand the movies you watch better?

# SCENE 2:

# THE HISTORY OF LEADERSHIP

———

*"These are facts, sir. Not schoolbook history, not Mr. Wells' history, but history nevertheless. They sent this foot-high jeweled bird to Charles, who was then in Spain. They sent it in a galley commanded by a member of the Order. It never reached Spain."*
—KASPER GUTMAN, *THE MALTESE FALCON*

Failures of leadership are one reason we need to know the history of leadership.

Philosopher George Santayana is known to have said, "Those who cannot remember the past are condemned to repeat it."

Looking back at the history of leadership helps us to understand what has happened. It also helps us avoid the atrocities and missteps we could take if we are not careful.

What does the history of leadership look like? To begin, we need to get an understanding of what leadership *is*. If we do not know what leadership is, we cannot clearly look at its history.

Merriam-Webster has many definitions of leadership. They range from:

"a position as a leader of a group, organization, etc.,"

to

"the time when a person holds the position of leader,"

or, probably the best definition the Merriam-Webster dictionary provides is,

"the power or ability to lead other people."

Even the best definition in the dictionary is a poor idea of what leadership is, though.

John Maxwell, a Horatio Alger Award winner and the author of over seventy-five best-selling books on leadership, said, "Leadership is influence, nothing more, nothing less." What a great definition. When you think about movies, movies definitely have an influence over the viewer.

# Leadership is influence, nothing more, nothing less.

—JOHN C. MAXWELL

However, the influence of leadership can be positive or negative. There's always an impact. With that in mind, if we look at the history of leadership, we can better understand what leadership is and how it impacts us.

To begin, let's look at a few of the ways leaders have failed in their responsibilities.

Looking back throughout history, we see the importance of leadership starting from the beginning. We see a failure of leadership on the part of Adam in the Biblical story of Adam and Eve. Adam receives the authority to lead and watch over the Garden of Eden. Eve was to be his helper. Things went horribly wrong.

God had given a commandment that Adam could eat of any of the plants in the Garden except one. Adam could not eat the fruit from the tree of knowledge of good and evil. This was a commandment from on high—one he followed until he made a misstep in his leadership.

God also created Eve to be a helpmate. She was. Until the evil serpent tempted her. She ate of the tree of good and evil. She then presented the fruit to her husband, Adam. At this point, he had a choice. He could choose to lead and reject the offer of the fruit. Or he could take and eat of the fruit. Adam chose to follow instead of lead and ate the fruit his wife offered.

This was the first failure of leadership. There would be many more failures of leadership. We're now going to look at a wide-ranging variety of leadership failures. These examples are going to be from the history of the world, in governmental settings and the business world.

British King Vortigern had a horrendous leadership failure. In 440 A.D., he devised a plan to stop the raiding Picts and Scots. Instead of building up his military might, he outsourced the defense of his country. He chose the Saxons, Angles, and their allies. He believed this would ensure the safety of Britain. Instead, the Saxons discovered Britain had no military might. There were no defenses. They could attack and overtake Britain. They did.

Even George Washington failed in his leadership. Washington was given command of 300 men. They were ordered to protect Ohio country settlers from the aggressive French troops. Washington was given information by an Indian ally named Tanacharison. Tanacharison told Washington the French had a military force of over 1,000 troops. In response, Washington took refuge and built Fort Necessity.

Washington was goaded into attacking a thirty-two-member French delegation that was meeting.

Together, Washington and Tanacharison surrounded the delegation and attacked. Many of the delegation met an untimely death. Twenty-two members were taken captive.

The French did not take kindly to this act of aggression. Fort Necessity was weak and did not have the resources to repel an aggressive attack. The French eventually attacked, and Washington suffered great losses. Leading to his surrender.

Or, what about the greatest recent governmental leadership failure? We can assume correctly that the atrocities committed by Hitler in World War II could mark the greatest leadership failure. Signed shortly after World War I, the Treaty of Versailles contained wording that should have prohibited Germany from creating a mighty military. However, it was a poorly kept secret that Germany was looking to arm itself and create a military might to be reckoned with. Hitler let the world know that Germany had begun to grow its army and had created an air force. The leaders of the free world failed to act, and the world would soon be thrust into World War II.

An example of a business leadership failure is the Enron implosion. Enron filed for bankruptcy in November 2001. Because of the negligence and abuse of the top Enron officials, Enron collapsed upon itself and one of the greatest business scandals in recent memory happened. There were moral failings at the top of the organization. Leadership borrowed with no intent to repay; they manipulated energy prices and used unethical financial practices to boost the appearance of earnings.

Enron would never recover from the deceit and unethical practices of their leadership team. Team members, investors, and business associates are still reeling from the impact of these practices. The corrupt leadership at Enron impacted many beyond the walls of the organization.

History has given us examples of good and bad leaders. I have already covered the leadership of Adam, King Vortigern, George Washington, the world powers when it came to Hitler, and the poor leadership at Enron. These examples showed the failures of multiple leaders throughout the course of history. Of course, not all leaders are failures. We should also look at the history of successful leaders and what they have done to make the world a better place.

One of the first positive examples of leaders that I think of is the Chinese military general Sun Tzu. He was a military general from 500 B.C. You may not think much of him, but his leadership ideas are still being used today. Sun Tzu authored the book *The Art of War*. *The Art of War* was also translated into a made-for-television documentary movie looking at the ways Sun Tzu's principles have been used throughout history.

As a military leader, he had great insight into advancing over his adversaries. However, his ideas conflict with many modern leaders' ideas about leadership. *The Art of War* focused not on using military might to win the battle. Instead, Sun Tzu wrote about using political policies and strategies to prevent war, not enter them. This strategy differed from the idea of attacking fast and furiously until your opponent could no longer fight. Sun Tzu's strategies encouraged working through problems rather than fighting through them.

In *The Darkest Hour*, a movie about Winston Churchill's leadership through some of the darkest days of his time as a leader, Sir Anthony Eden reminds Churchill of the enormous task Churchill faced. Churchill had the weight of a country on his shoulders. The weight was almost too much.

However, Churchill knew he couldn't lead England alone. He decided to put together a war cabinet to go over their options. He chose not only people who would agree with his ideas but also people he knew would strongly disagree and pushback. He knew his war cabinet would be stronger with people who could stand up to him. In a great moment in this film, Churchill knew he couldn't get the Navy ships he needed to Dunkirk. Instead, Churchill decided to do a Hail Mary. He called on the citizens of Dunkirk to come together. Operation Dynamo called on civilians to come to the aid of the people of Dunkirk by bringing their boats to Dunkirk and ferrying people away.

Sun Tzu and Churchill were both historical figures from the past. Many great leaders shape history—we need also to look at the present.

If we're looking at modern leaders, we have to look at Mother Teresa. She was a lowly Catholic nun who changed the hearts and minds of many people. Mother Teresa committed her life to ending the suffering of the world's poor. She did this through giving up her desires and working for the needs of others. The world saw great results from her actions.

During the 1982 Siege of Beirut, Mother Teresa brokered a cease-fire between the two warring factions, the Israeli army and Palestinian guerrillas. This temporary cease-fire allowed for the rescue of thirty-seven children from a hospital. Not only did Mother Teresa help broker the cease-fire, but she also went out to the front lines with the Red Cross to evacuate the children.

She continued her humanitarian work until her death in 1997. She may have passed away, but her legacy lives on. People still carry on Mother Teresa's vision and work today. In 2016, the Catholic church recognized Mother Teresa as a saint.

There's no steadfast rule about leadership and what leaders can do. Leaders come in all shapes and sizes. They can be fantastic leaders who help people grow. They can help their countries thrive and survive. Businesses boom because of leaders willing to work hard, smart, and with integrity. On the flip side, there are bad leaders. These leaders look out for themselves. They seek a way to reap the benefits and leave everyone else behind. We saw this with the Enron corruption.

Throughout the rest of this book, we are going to look at ways we can find the positive leadership values of leaders in movies. I already shared one. The story of Winston Churchill came from my viewing of the movie *The Darkest Hour*. The movie opened a window into the world Churchill was experiencing during the attack on Dunkirk. *The Darkest Hour* was full of leadership lessons. So are many other movies that we watch on a regular basis.

It is easy for me to rattle off a list of movies with leadership lessons. I believe every movie contains at least **one** leadership lesson. Throughout this book, we're going to look at movies that have impacted other leaders and their leadership styles. We're also going to get a glimpse into the minds of movie writers such as David Hayter (the writer for *X-Men 1* and *2*), Daniel Knudsen, and others. Most movies contain multiple lessons we can discover if only we look through the window we're given into a new world.

That's what the next chapter will discuss. We will look at how movies are a window into a new world.

The ideas presented there may shock and amaze you. Or you may already be a *Reel Leader* and know that movies open a window that helps us see things in a way we never thought to see.

## DISCUSSION QUESTIONS:

1. What surprised you about the history of leadership?
2. Do you find yourself making any of the failures previous leaders have made?
3. What can you learn from the failures of the leaders who have come before you?
4. How do you want your history of leadership to be remembered?

## SCENE 3:

# THE SCIENCE OF LEARNING

———

*"Remember what happened to Galileo? They threw him in jail because he said the earth was not the center of the universe. That could happen to us."*

—DR. SID, *FINAL FANTASY: THE SPIRITS WITHIN*

Have you ever thought about the way we learn? Most of us haven't thought about this since we graduated from high school. Maybe even before.

### WHAT IS THE SCIENCE OF LEARNING?

The Merriam-Webster dictionary defines learning in three distinct ways. The first is *to gain knowledge or understanding of, or skill in, by study, instruction, or experience.* Another definition from the Merriam-Webster dictionary is *to come to realize or be able.* The last one is *to acquire knowledge or skill or a behavioral tendency.* All three are great definitions of learning. They help us understand what learning is and how it impacts us.

We learn to gain knowledge in a specific field of study or skill. We do this by studying, instruction, or experience. I believe this means we learn from the movies we watch. We can learn leadership from movies by studying characters, looking for the moral premise, and experiencing the emotional roller-coaster movies provide. Each movie we watch can bring us closer to the leader we want to be. We can grow as we watch!

The science of learning doesn't rope us into one way of learning. It doesn't even stop us from discovering ways of doing things through non-traditional methods. In fact, this is one of the greatest ways of learning. The non-traditional method of learning is something we're going to lean heavily into with *Reel Leadership.*

When we're able to look at something others ignored and see the potential within this tool to teach us something, we're going to leapfrog past our competition. If we can grasp the concept of learning from the movies, we can develop a way of leading that takes us past other leaders. Learning from the movies means you're not handcuffed to the old style of teaching. You're able to break the shackles that hold many leaders back. What an advantage you'll gain.

Watching a movie, seeing the leadership principles in the movie, and then applying them to the way you lead is a way of learning. This also helps you to cement the leadership principles you see in movies into your everyday leadership tasks.

Isn't that awesome? I think so. I hope you will come to believe the same as we dive deeper into what it means to learn in this chapter. It might surprise you how easily you can apply the lessons you see in a movie to the way you lead.

Don't be afraid to jump into this chapter. We're going to look at the ways we learn and the principles behind learning. Discovering how these apply to leadership is fun and engaging. It definitely opened my eyes. I hope the following words in this chapter will illuminate your path as well.

## THE WAYS WE LEARN

Have you ever thought about the way we learn? Most of us haven't thought about this since we graduated from high school. Maybe even before.

When you were in elementary school, you might remember all the different exercises they encouraged you to do in your learning process. These exercises included using different senses.

Teachers encouraged you to look at your surrounding environment. You took in new ideas and sights through your vision.

You were then encouraged to listen. Did you hear how that red-wing blackbird sounded different from the woodpecker? This engaged our hearing.

Next, they encouraged you to take in a deep breath through your nose. What smells did you smell? You might have smelled musty feathers or the woodchips in the birdcage.

Finally, they encouraged you to pet the bird. The feathers were smooth on one bird. Another bird had slightly rougher feathers.

There is a fifth sense with taste, but the teacher didn't ask you to eat the bird! That would be just wrong, right? Unless it was chicken.

Using multiple senses helped you to learn more about the environment around you. You understood the bird better. You could describe the scents, sounds, look, and feel of the birds. Most of your senses were engaged. This made for a better learning experience.

Now think about movies. They engage all our senses. The movies we watch can help us better understand the world.

Now think about movies. They engage all our senses. The movies we watch can help us better understand the world.

Engaging your senses is better known as active learning. According to Learn Through Experience, an experiential educational database housing an extensive listing of experiential education programs, active learning helps students and adults recall and associate.

There's also experiential learning. Experiential learning engages students with a hands-on learning experience. This type of learning engages all the senses. They state that "incorporating the senses in a multisensory manner activates more of the brain and allows students the skills necessary to succeed."

**PRINCIPLES OF LEARNING**

iEduNote, a website about learning by Shadhin Kangal, takes the ideas of the five senses one step further. They say there are five principles of learning.

Much like the five senses, the five principles of learning are guidelines to how people learn most effectively. By including more of these principles in your training, the more effective the training will be.

What are the five principles of learning? They are:

**Participation –**

As noted earlier in the chapter, senses are a vital part of learning. When we engage the senses, we engage a learning trigger in our minds. The same principle applies when we take part in active learning.

Touching, smelling, hearing, seeing, and tasting are all parts of active learning. Many of these senses are also engaged when we watch a film. We are **watching** a moving picture. We are **hearing** the sounds of the movie. We may **smell** the environment around us (while not a part of the movie itself, these smells trigger our memory later). Are you eating pop-corn? If you are, this is also an experience that engages the sense of **taste**.

You are taking part in watching a movie more than you think!

## Repetition –

Whenever we repeat an activity, we cement the actions into our subconscious. We create muscle memories of the actions we need to take.

Now, think of the movies you love. How many times have you seen the movie *Dumb & Dumber* starring Jim Carey and Jeff Daniels? There are probably lines you can repeat straight from memory because of your repeated watching.

One of those for me is, "Just when I think you couldn't pos-sibly be any dumber, you go and do something like this... **AND TOTALLY REDEEM YOURSELF!**"

These repeated viewings help us remember what the movies are trying to teach us. They help us remember the *moral premise* (which I mentioned in the introduction), as Will Smith's screenwriter, Stan Williams, calls the major, over-arching premises of movies. We are working out the muscle of our minds.

## Relevance –

Another principle of learning is the principle of relevance. The more relevant the topic, the more meaningful the learning becomes. We remember because the topic is meaningful to us.

Imagine if you recently jumped to a conclusion in your work. You had what you thought was all the correct information. You based your judgment and actions on the information you received. You then discover the information was faulty.

Ugh...

It's hard to realize you acted on misinformation.

You then watch the movie *Nobody*. It is an action-revenge film starring Bob Odenkirk as a seemingly nobody named Hutch. Someone burglarizes his house. As if that is not bad enough, he fails to take a swing at the burglars when he has a chance.

This disappoints his family.

Hutch's daughter comes to him. She tells him the burglars stole her kitty cat bracelet during the robbery. This sends Hutch into a violent spiral where he confronts the robbers and takes out a large portion of the Russian mob.

Then, Hutch discovers something as he's about to burn his basement.

His daughter's kitty cat bracelet had fallen under the basement couch. He was acting on misinformation.

Seeing this play out on the big screen after you recently made the same mistake helps you to remember the lesson because it applies to a situation you recently experienced. You remember to examine the information you've received to make sure you're not acting on wrong information.

**Transference –**

Transference is the act of transferring what you've learned into actual application. You have seen and experienced a learning experience. Now, what do you do with it?

We can take the example above from the movie *Nobody*. It is relevant, but you have yet to transfer the leadership idea into practice. How do you transfer this lesson?

The next time a team member brings you information about a situation, you thank them for the information. You then begin to examine what they told you. You may research deeper into the issue. You may come back and ask for more information. This time, you didn't jump to a conclusion. You researched the situation. And you discovered the information was incorrect. You've now avoided a mess.

By digging deeper, you are now **using** the lesson you learned from *Nobody*. You have begun to *transfer* the lesson to your leadership toolbox.

**Feedback –**

The last principle of learning is feedback or, said in another way, reflection. Feedback is the processing of information regarding your progress. I believe we can extend this to a different kind of feedback in relation to film.

Whenever we see a great movie, we love to talk and discuss the film. We love to go into the details of how Sub-Zero killed Scorpion in *Mortal Kombat* and how Scorpion came to finish off Sub-Zero in the end. Or how Spider-Man had trouble learning to web sling when he first gained his powers. He was clumsy and awkward as he swung across New York City.

These discussions are feedback too. They help us remember what happened and how they relate to our everyday lives.

As you can see, movies are an excellent way to learn. They meet all the criteria mentioned by iEduNote. Could movies be the ultimate learning tool? We will see...

## DISCUSSION QUESTIONS:

1. How does the science of learning tie into the way you lead?
2. What principles of learning have you overlooked? What would happen if you began to incorporate these principles into your leadership?
3. Do you use repetition in the way you communicate? Do you see a benefit in repeating yourself?
4. Are you receiving feedback from your team? How can you encourage your team to give you more feedback?

# SCENE 4:

# WHY NOW?

---

*"When a defining moment comes along, you can do one of two things: Define the moment, or let the moment define you.*
—ROY MCAVOY, *TIN CUP*

I think back to when I began my journey of personal development. I wanted to become the best leader that I could. Everywhere I looked, I saw successful people telling me how to become a better, more successful leader.

I looked at their lives. I saw the proof in the pudding. These guys appeared to be the real deal. I won't say they weren't. I believe they are. Their wisdom has gotten me to where I am today. These men and women are one reason I began my blog and the place where I formed the ideas for *Reel Leadership*.

I am ever grateful for the wisdom and knowledge these men and women shared with me. I'm especially thankful for the encouragement by Dan Miller, the author of *48 Days to The Work You Love*, to begin my own blog where I could share the leadership insights I had gleaned from them, my time in leadership, and the people who have been great leaders in my life.

However, something was missing in what they shared with their audience. They gave extremes of one side while ignoring the middle ground. We all do this. There's no faulting someone for sharing their extreme. Extreme examples catch our attention and force us to evaluate what we are doing. Yet I believe their extremes hurt me. More importantly, I believe their extremes are hurting you like they hurt me. When we use extremes to teach a lesson, we begin to alienate those we teach.

Leading experts in the fields of personal development and leadership doled out advice to avoid all forms of entertainment. These experts used their platforms such as podcasts, TED Talks, and conferences to share the message that entertainment is bad. In lieu of entertainment, they gave me advice on what to do. Instead of music, listen to podcasts during your commute. This is what the late, great Zig Ziglar called Automobile University. This would allow you to put positive information into your mind during your daily commute, which could be upward of two to three hours of positive content every day.

Other advice given was to give up reading fiction books. Instead of fiction books, begin to read non-fiction books. The non-fiction books would fill your mind with new knowledge. You could learn from the greatest minds of the world. Great men and women have written fantastic books full of everything they knew at the time. Access this wealth of information we are given. It's better than those candy-for-the-mind fiction books.

One other piece of advice given was to give up watching television shows and movies. They presented research that showed the most successful people watched very little television and even fewer movies. These forms of entertainment were garbage for the mind. They had no redeeming value. They were only a waste of time. Instead, fill your time watching great TED Talks and motivational training programs. These would inspire you to be better.

Do you know what I did? I listened to these men and women I respected. I stopped listening to my punk rock and hardcore music during my drives. I replaced them with uplifting podcasts such as *The Positive University Podcast* by Jon Gordon, *48 Days* by Dan Miller, and the *Andy Stanley Leadership Podcast*. During my drives to the office, I felt myself growing in knowledge. I was becoming a more successful leader.

Or so I thought.

Do you know what else I did? I stopped reading fiction books. I gave up reading *Star Wars* novels by Timothy Zahn. The *Lord of The Rings* trilogy by J.R.R. Tolkien? Nope, couldn't read that book. Anything that wasn't personal development or leadership focused was off the bookshelf for me. I began reading *The Compound Effect* by Darren Hardy. There was also *The 7 Habits of Highly Effective People* by Stephen R. Covey. I added Simon Sinek's *Start with Why* to my reading list. *How to Win Friends and Influence People* by Dale Carnegie? Yes, please. Let's devour that book.

I'm growing! I'm becoming the best version of myself I can be....

Or so I thought.

Last but not least, I kissed television shows and movies good-bye. There would be no more *Pirates of the Caribbean: The Curse of the Black Pearl* in my house. I wasn't going to watch *Die Hard* 1, 2, or 3 again! *The Expendables*? Watching them was expendable. Movies and television shows weren't going to drag me down anymore. I was replacing these mindless forms of entertainment with better content. I would watch Brené Brown's TED Talk on daring greatly. I would purchase a membership for Michael Nichol's Guidestone University. I would devour the leadership videos contained within the university.

All of this to make me a better leader....

Or so I thought.

An interesting thing began to happen as I devoured all this new, positive, encouraging content. I began to discover every one of these thought leaders had something in common. They **loved** the use of stories to teach their lessons. They would use lessons from their own lives, from the lives of the people they knew, and they would even tell fictional stories. A repeating byline began to emerge. Soon, everyone was talking about how *stories stick, stats don't.*

Gasp. Gulp. Say what?

Yes, that's right... These thought leaders who encouraged people to avoid content that wasn't considered motivational or uplifting were telling stories.

A switch had flipped.

I realized something. **MOVIES** are stories. They are telling the viewer something. We only have to pay attention. If we pay attention to the moral premises and hidden ideas presented in movies, we could learn from these stories.

This brings me to why I am writing this book. It goes beyond my sadness of the time I lost in avoiding so much of what I enjoy. I missed the enjoyment of going out to the movies with my friends or family. I missed time chatting with others about the concepts presented in the latest blockbuster movie. I missed figuring out why I enjoyed a movie or why I disliked a movie.

The why behind *Reel Leadership* is this: I don't want you to fall victim to the thinking to which I fell victim. I don't want you to miss out on the activities you enjoy in life. I don't want you to miss out on all the fantastic movies Hollywood is putting out.

I want you to head to your local cinema and purchase a ticket. I want you to purchase a bucket of popcorn and add the nacho cheddar powder to your tasty snack. I want you to head to your comfortable reclining theater seat and take a seat with pride. I want you to hold your head up high when you leave the theater. If someone asks you what you did this past weekend, I want you to tell them, "I went to the movie theater. I enjoyed a nice buttery bucket of popcorn. I watched my new favorite film. I walked out with a couple of new leadership ideas as well." All of this without any shameful feelings.

You don't have to be ashamed of watching a movie, like I did when I would *screw up* and go off track. You don't have to sneak in a movie because you're scared of what someone may think of you.

It's time we begin to accept movies for what they are. Movies today are the modern-day fable. They are new tellings of Aesop's fable "The Hare and The Tortoise" or George Orwell's *Animal Farm* or Jonathan Swift's *Gulliver's Travels*. The fables of old were fun, engaging, and entertaining stories. They helped us discover truth in fiction. So are today's movies.

## Movies are the modern-day fable.

I want to encourage you to think of movies as visual fables. They are telling stories that move the mind, body, and soul. They can touch you emotionally, spiritually, and even physically. There is power in movies.

I remember the first time I realized movies were a powerful teaching tool. I was preparing a lesson for my youth group. I was trying to come up with a lesson. The struggle was real, as I couldn't find anything to talk about. I kept pushing myself to get something out there and couldn't. Then I began to think about one of my favorite movies, *Star Wars*.

*Star Wars* is full of lessons we can discover. These lessons go the gamut. *Star Wars* has life lessons. *Star Wars* has leadership lessons. And, *Star Wars* has spiritual lessons.

One of the faith lessons I pulled from *Star Wars* was the power of sacrifice.

Jesus tells His followers in John 15:13, "No one has greater love than this, to lay down one's life for one's friends."

This is a common theme throughout the *Star Wars* films. Specifically, in *Star Wars Episode 4: The Empire Strikes Back*, we see Obi-Wan Kenobi sacrifice his life for his friends.

Obi-Wan battles his former protégé, Darth Vader (though when Obi-Wan was training him, Darth Vader was Anakin Skywalker). Luke Skywalker, Princess Leia, and Han Solo are rushing to escape from the Death Star. Obi-Wan sees his friends trying to escape. He knows he has to make a sacrifice. He stops fighting Darth Vader and allows Darth Vader to kill him. This gives the trio time to escape and fight another day.

I want you to continue to having experiences like this. I want you to understand that movies are not mindless entertainment. Movies are things we can enjoy while growing ourselves.

Let's face it. The world is screaming at us that screen time is bad time. We're told constantly to put away the phone, shut off the TV, or dim the screen. However, screen time is not the problem. It is the overuse of screens and the way we view them.

Screen time with movies can provide valuable leadership insights into the world you lead in. We have to be careful not to overindulge, but screen time is not necessarily bad. Screen time can be a significant benefit to the way you learn.

As we continue through *Reel Leadership*, we are going to see how movies can help us understand leadership principles in a new light. It is time for us to stop maligning movies. It is now time for us to accept movies as a valuable leadership training tool.

## DISCUSSION QUESTIONS:

1. What negative associations have you had with movies?
2. What positive associations have you had with movies?
3. How has a movie impacted the way you viewed leadership?
4. Do you think screen time is bad time? Why or why not?

# SCENE 5:

# A MORAL PREMISE?

---

*"I watch movies, and I really try to analyze them. And I write out these moral premise statements. So, I can share with other filmmakers as we're developing story ideas, like what works with the audience."*

—DANIEL KNUDSEN

Daniel Knudsen is an actor, director, producer, writer, and more in the film industry. He has starred in over ten roles in film. He has directed eleven titles. He has nine producer credits to his name. And he's written three projects.

In a discussion I had with Knudsen, he broke open the idea of *Reel Leadership*. There's a terminology that the film industry uses for what *Reel Leadership* explores. The film industry calls the lessons in movies the "moral premise." Knudsen learned this from Will Smith's screenwriter.

Knudsen says screenwriter Dr. Stan Williams coined the term "moral premise," and Knudsen shared a few examples of the moral premise of movies we may know. The movies don't even have to focus on our demographic. Whether we feel we are too old, are not romantic, or don't like to be scared, all movies can portray a moral premise, or leadership lesson.

A great example of this is *Frozen*. Knudsen had this to say about *Frozen*: "And it's fun because it's kind of like going underneath the hood. We see a movie like *Frozen*. And we're guys and we're millennials, we're too 'out of the age range or even the target demographic that it is made for,' but it still speaks to us. Why is that? It's because of the truth of the moral premise found within that narrative."

> It's because of the truth of the moral premise found within that narrative (why movies can speak to us even if we're not the target audience).

—DANIEL KNUDSEN

A great example of a movie with a moral premise is the film *Signs* by M. Night Shyamalan. Knudsen shared details about a conversation he had with Christian author Michael Heizer about the movie *Signs*. Heizer said instead of telling people to go read a couple of chapters on systematic theology, he tells them to just go watch *Signs* because of the moral premise in the movie.

The moral premise of *Signs* is that believing in atheism leads to pessimism and isolation. We see this with Mel Gibson's character. He rejects the idea of divine order in the world. He becomes increasingly pessimistic. The more pessimistic he becomes, the more isolated he becomes from his family, in his own relationships. It's a vicious cycle that brings the man down.

The flip side is different. When Gibson's character turns the moral premise corner, we see that believing in Divine Order leads to hope and relationships and relational community. By the end of the movie, he has a closer relationship with his family. He's made amends and grown.

Or we can look at the movie *Frozen*. *Frozen* is an animated children's move that tells the story of two sisters, Anna and Elsa. Elsa develops powers with which she can control cold. These powers are scary, and Elsa secludes herself. She shies away from people and anything she may hurt.

According to Knudsen, Elsa and Anna and the idea of being paranoid or reckless illustrate the moral premise. Elsa is paranoid about using her powers. She's afraid of the damage she could unleash if she let her powers out. On the other hand, you have Anna, who is reckless. Yet, these two things lead to the same thing. Paranoia and recklessness lead to danger and separation. We see this throughout the narrative of *Frozen*.

We also see the flip side of this. Knudsen continues with the moral premise of *Frozen*. The flip side, or the dangerous side of the characters in *Frozen*, is that when we learn balanced power, it leads to stability and community.

Another powerful example of the moral premise in film is from the movie *The Greatest Showman*. Here, we have

Hugh Jackman playing PT Barnum. PT Barnum builds up a huge facade. This leads to dissatisfaction and loneliness. He becomes isolated and unhappier the deeper he goes into the persona he has created. In *The Greatest Showman,* the flip side to this premise is that when you build an identity on authenticity, it leads to satisfaction and family. PT Barnum comes to embrace this truth at the end with the characters who are like those in the island of misfits.

What does all of this have to do with leadership lessons and movies? I believe it has *everything* to do with finding leadership lessons in movies. When we realize screenwriters, directors, and producers are placing moral premises into movies, it's easy to understand they are also placing great leadership lessons into the movies we're watching or want to watch. In fact, I think a moral premise is a leadership lesson.

This idea is going to be explored more throughout the book. We're going to see how the moral premise and direction the movie producer takes impacts the way films touch us. There are reasons behind the film. We only have to look at them with eyes open to the message contained within.

## DISCUSSION QUESTIONS:

1. Have you looked for a moral premise in movies before?
2. How does the idea of a moral premise change the way you think about movies?
3. What moral premise have you subconsciously noticed in movies?
4. How can you look for moral premises in the movies you watch going forward?

## SCENE 6:

# MOVIES ARE A WINDOW

———

*"You know what I'm craving? A little perspective. That's it. I'd like some fresh, clear, well-seasoned perspective. Can you suggest a good wine to go with that?*

—ANTON EGO, *RATATOUILLE*

What if I told you movies were a window to the world around you?

Every movie opens a window to a world of which you may not be a part. The writers, directors, and producers of movies are looking for ways to open the moviegoer's eyes to an unknown world.

I remember watching *Jurassic Park* at the Cinema Carousel. I was young, and my mother accompanied me. We sat in the front row of the theater showing the movie. We were ready to see dinosaurs brought to life and, maybe, be thrilled just a little bit. This happened, but something else happened along the way.

Movies opened my eyes to a new world—a world that connected my personal world with the power of storytelling in movies.

We sat, enthralled in the movie, not knowing what would come next. We saw dinosaurs come to life. Then, the action on the screen terrified my mom as one of the dinosaurs made a threatening move. She jumped and gasped in terror.

This moment, though I didn't realize it at the time, began my journey of reel leadership.

I look back on this incident as the impetus of learning to see more in movies. I can see how *Jurassic Park* scaring my mom is a key moment in my reel leadership journey. It cemented the power of movies to move us (literally and metaphorically). When I look back on this moment, I see what movies can do to us. It now helps me understand how movies touch us. Because of that, I can see that movies can also teach us.

If a movie can connect our emotions to what is happening on the screen, could movies move us in a more meaningful way as well? I've discovered over the last several years that this is true. Movies connect us and draw us into a world in which we have never been a part, such as what happened with my mother. As she was watching the movie, something connected her to the action. When the dinosaur surprised us, it truly surprised her.

But there are other ways movies can touch us. They connect with our emotions and our brains. We try to figure out what Liam Neeson's character in *The Honest Thief* will do next. Or we try to understand what motivated the villain, Gollum, in *The Lord of the Rings*.

Movies are an open window we have to be willing to walk through.

I was reading an article on the website Relevant. The story was by a man named Brett McCracken. He's someone I've known through the Christian music and writing industry. It shocked me to see him cover the topic of movies and why we watch them.

The insights he offered in his article were fascinating. They resonated with me. I realized how impactful movies could be and are.

## Movies are an open window we have to be willing to walk through.

The first point McCracken made was that **art is a window**. Try as they may, people disparage movies and try to claim movies are not an art form, but they're wrong. Movies are art. They can touch the soul and move the spirit.

Think of the movie *Toy Story 3*. It's the story of young Andy growing up and heading off to college. He packs up his toys to be placed in the attic, but his mom makes a terrible mistake. She believes the toys were to be donated. A wild journey ensues with the toys ending up at the Sunnyside Daycare. During the climax of the movie, the toys are sent to an incinerator. The toys brace themselves for what is coming. Holding hands as they inch closer to the fire, they're ready for their destruction. Thankfully, they're rescued by the alien toys from the skill claw game. Eventually, the toys find their way back to Andy's house.

Woody writes a note to Andy. The note convinces Andy to give his toys to a young girl named Bonnie. Andy boxes up the toys and gives Bonnie the toys. Before he leaves, he tells Bonnie about each toy.

At this point, those of us who grew up with *Toy Story* are bawling our eyes out. We've seen the toys that have been a part of a great movie series almost die, then we see Andy do something we've all had to do: Say goodbye to our beloved toys.

So, why should we consider movies to be art? Art is created to move people, to touch their emotions, to make them feel something. *Toy Story 3* and other movies do this. There's no doubt about it. There's no denying that movies are an art form. They're also something else.

McCracken mentions C.S. Lewis, the author of *The Lion, the Witch, and the Wardrobe* , in his article. Lewis wrote in *An Experiment in Criticism* that we "seek an enlargement of our being. We want to be more than ourselves. Each of us, by nature, sees the whole world from one point of view with a perspective and a selectiveness peculiar to himself.... We want to see with other eyes, to imagine with other imaginations, to feel with other hearts, as well as with our own.... We demand windows."

Movies open a large window to our lives and the lives of those around us. Movies become a window into the lives of those we don't know and normally wouldn't have any reason to interact with.

Think about the diverse movies you have watched. Are there any that make you see a group of people in a new light? Have you felt challenged by the experiences of someone in a film? I have.

*The Little Things* starring Denzel Washington and Rami Malek is a great example. This film brings the viewer into the world of an African American cop who made a mistake and is paying the price for it. However, because of his ethnicity, we see the unfairness of his treatment. It's a window into the world of injustice around us. We may never see the injustice, but those around us may experience it. This helps us understand our world is not all there is.

Or what about *The Marksman* with Liam Neeson? Neeson's character Jim becomes entangled with a mother and son who crossed the USA-Mexico border illegally. Their plight is front and center as they are fleeing from the blood-thirsty cartel. We're thrust into a world of which we may not be aware. *The Marksman* shows the dangers those fleeing to the United States may face.

Whether it is the prejudice of immigrants or the struggle in legally crossing the border, people face many issues others will never experience. Once again, each movie becomes another window into a world we don't know.

What does this mean for you and your leadership? It means we can see things from a new point of view. We can, as C.S. Lewis puts it, see with a new set of eyes.

But how? How does this work?

As we watch movies, they draw us into the action, the story, or another factor of the movie. Through action, story, and music, they draw us to the window of someone else's life and viewpoints. They show us *their* viewpoints.

If we're intentional, we can look at their window and understand the viewpoints of others. It's a way to learn about others without truly interacting with them. We can begin to understand the why behind the actions of others.

What window are you looking through?

Brett McCracken wrote, "Movies are different because they can capture, probe, explore the world in ways no other medium can. We feel the texture of a silk dress in a costume drama like *Bright Star*. We smell the blood spurting off of a smoking bullet in *Inglourious Basterds*. We languish at the sight of a tormented face in a movie like *Precious* or *The Road*—every line and wrinkle of which the camera so painfully exploits. Movies are visceral."

And this is why movies are such a great way to explore leadership and interpersonal relationships. Movies are visceral. They draw viewers into the presentation.

If there is a story to be told, the medium of film can tell it.

Through movies, the story can grab us and pull us in like a tractor beam in *Star Trek*. In *Star Trek*, tractor beams use a gravitonal force beam to manipulate objects outside of a ship. The tractor beams in *Star Trek* are typically used to pull and guide other spacecraft to docking stations. The story, in movies, is our real-life tractor beam. It locks onto us and pulls us deeper and deeper.

We have to allow the tractor beam of movies to pull us into the window that is now open. We can learn from the movies we watch and explore. We also have to be willing to fight against the pull of the tractor beam.

Movie producers and writers want to pull us in a specific direction. Many times, it is purely for entertainment's sake. Sometimes it is more than that.

Yet, you have the power to direct where you go while watching a movie.

Will you watch a movie purely for entertainment's sake? Will you do it to kill two hours of your day? Or will you be intentional and let the tractor beam pull you toward a more meaningful viewing experience?

I propose we let the tractor beam pull us in and guide us to the important lessons contained in the movie. You can do this, but you have to be willing to direct yourself.

Where have you let the tractor beam pull you? Is it to where you need to be? What can you do to redirect from the direction you're heading? Could you change the trajectory and find yourself at a point where you're learning and growing from this source of entertainment?

We have to be intentional. We have to direct ourselves to the learning side of movies.

When we do this, we can begin exploring the deeper meanings of movies.

As McCracken shared, we can explore worlds in which we've never been. We can see things in ways we never expected to see. We can also see through fresh eyes.

Let the big screen impact you.

See that movies are more than just a quick escape. They are not there simply to numb our minds and help us forget what is happening around us. Movies are deeper and more profound than this—especially when we look for the important leadership lessons in movies.

Over ten years ago, a new window opened in my world after watching movies more closely. I began looking at them through the lens of leadership. Now, I can't shut this window. Once the window opened, it remained open and in more than just the realm of movies.

I want to open a window for you. I want you to look through the window I've been looking through for more than ten years. This window will open your eyes and help you see there's more to movies. They can more than entertain you.

You can find important lessons in what many people consider mundane entertainment.

*Reel Leadership* will be that window for you as you read through the book. It will open your eyes to many leadership lessons you have missed during your movie-watching days. Prepare to look through a new window.

## DISCUSSION QUESTIONS:

1. What movie has had a major impact on you? What did you notice that was different?
2. How has a movie made you look at the world differently? Why did it have this impact?
3. How do you view movies—as a simple escape or as a way to find out more about someone else?
4. What needs to change about the way you look at screen time and movies?

# ACT 2

## SCENE 7:

# YOU NEED A HOOK

———

*"I'll be back."*
—ARNOLD SCHWARZENEGGER, *THE TERMINATOR* (1984)

Have you been there?

You're sitting in a dark theater. The movie starts. You're all excited to watch a great story. Then, nothing happens.

For hours, the story, or the lack of, drags on. You wonder when you can get up and leave. Maybe you even do!

I've seen a few of these movies. I've wanted to leave after fifteen to thirty minutes because *nothing* happens. The movie is a dud. Nothing kept me enthralled with the story.

I remember this with the comic book-based movie *Ghost Rider*. It starred Nicolas Cage as Johnny Blaze/Ghost Rider. He was the Spirit of Vengeance. This movie should have been amaze-balls. Yet it was truly disappointing. I remember wanting to walk out of the theater within the first fifteen minutes. Unfortunately for me, I didn't walk out because I had paid good money to watch the film.

These movies lacked a hook. They didn't engage the audience. The audience either leaves or they tell others about their horrible experience.

Former screenwriter Patrick Lencioni said he learned that the most important part of writing a movie or the most important minutes of the movie are the first ten minutes.

This portion of the movie is called *the hook.*

Lencioni thinks of *Raiders of The Lost Ark* when he thinks of iconic movies. The first ten minutes of this movie set up a great sense of suspense and intrigue. A lot happens in this portion of the movie.

Indiana Jones goes in and takes the idol.

Things start going crazy.

He gets on a plane and there's a snake there.

Lots of great excitement follows.

Then, the movie transitions to Indiana Jones in his classroom, and it moves to a slower speed.

However, before slowing down, the story did something.

It pulled you in.

It hooked you.

*Ghost Rider* could have introduced a killer hook. The story is of a man who sells his soul to the devil. This transaction occurs because Johnny Blaze wants to save his father. His father is slowly dying of cancer. The devil sought out Johnny Blaze and offered him a deal to cure the cancer. Once his father's cancer is cured, the devil pulls one over on Johnny and his father dies anyway. This great hook happened too late into the movie for it to be effective.

Opening with this scene could have been a fantastic hook to engage audience members. Instead, you're left waiting and wanting to be pulled into the *Ghost Rider* movie. There was so much potential to drag you in, but they failed to land the hook.

But what does that really have to do with leadership?

Lencioni is one of the founders of The Table Group, a consulting firm based in California that focuses on corporate and organizational health. He is also the author of eleven books with over six million copies sold.

The man knows how to write and hook people.

He also hosts the *At the Table* podcast, a leadership podcast that gives you the opportunity to sit across the table from one of the world's greatest experts in leadership. In this program, he tackles various topics related to the world of work. It is a truly great listen for anyone who wants to expand their leadership skills.

In episode six, he and his co-host Cody Thompson discussed meetings and how leaders can make meetings more engaging. The conversation was fascinating. Their conversation revolved around the fact that people *hate* meetings. People are itching to get out of their seats after a twenty-to-thirty-minute meeting.

As Patrick Lencioni put it, "We are dooming our meetings to be boring."

However, people are glued to their seats when it comes to movies. Movies often run one and a half to two to even three or more hours. People love them. They don't want to leave, unlike the common meeting.

I think we can all agree that great movies have great hooks. The great movies use hooks to bring us into the movie and make us feel engaged.

## We are dooming our meetings to be boring.

—PATRICK LENCIONI

On the other hand, bad movies that fail to have a hook lose the audience. The audience, as in a bad meeting, becomes antsy and wants to leave.

Do leaders really need to have hooks?

Leaders need to lead with a hook because it will capture the attention of those they lead.

But remember, I don't mean the kind of hooks a boxer may throw. The hooks a leader needs are not that right hook you want to pummel Jerry in accounting with when he doesn't balance the budget properly. Throwing that kind of hook will probably get you a trip to the HR department, regardless of which level of leadership you're at. While it's not landing a physical right hook on a team member, leaders need to lead with a hook.

We need to hook our teams and that can happen over a variety of areas.

You need to hook the audience. But, who is your audience?

## HOOKING YOUR AUDIENCE

In this section we're going to discuss a couple of different audiences and the areas in which you need to have a hook. Some of these will be intuitive, others may make you scratch your head a little bit, but they are valuable tools for you as a leader to have.

### YOUR TEAM MEMBERS

The first audience you have are your team members. These are the people you are leading and interacting with on a regular basis.

Who are these people?

They're your direct reports, the ones with whom you have direct communication.

However, your audience is not limited to the workplace. More than your direct reports, your first audience may include your husband, wife, children, and more.

You are communicating to this audience through various mediums. It may be an email, a phone call, a text message, or the dreaded meeting. You need to make sure that you hold the attention of those you lead. One of your roles as a leader is to help your team engage in the mission and vision of the organization.

There's no better way to do this than to hook your team members.

If your team members are not buying into what your organization is doing, they're not going to give you their best work. They're going to struggle to come into work. They're going to struggle to give you their best. They're going to struggle to push you through those challenging times.

Let's take a minute to think about the movie *Saving Private Ryan.*

The movie opened with a powerful hook.

There is a quietness you don't expect as young men begin walking toward their death. The shelling begins and bodies begin to fall as American soldiers are trying to get to land.

That's a hook!

Now, imagine hooking your team with this kind of clarity in the mission and vision of your organization. They're going to become energized and engaged and ready to do the hard and challenging work that needs to be done to make the organization successful.

How do you hook your team with the mission and vision? Your mission and vision have to be able to connect your team to the purpose behind it all. You have to help your team see the impact your organization is making. You do this by giving exciting examples of what your product is doing to enhance the lives of those using it.

Let's look at the mission and vision at Zoom, the video conferencing company that boomed during the COVID-19 pandemic. Their mission and vision became crystal clear.

- The mission: to make video communications frictionless and secure.
- Their vision: to provide video communications empowering people to accomplish more.

Basically, Zoom wants to help businesses and organizations connect face-to-face while being apart.

Do you think the employees at Zoom were excited about the work they were doing during the COVID-19 pandemic?

The leaders of the organization can make a strong hook to engage their employees because it relates to what is going on in the world. They couldn't get away from the fact that their software platform was helping organizations continue during one of the most difficult times in global history.

**YOUR MEETING ATTENDEES**

The second audience we need to look at are the people to whom you present in the dreaded meetings. Meetings, as Patrick Lencioni mentioned in his podcast, are hated by most attendees. I even wrote a blog post about this where I shared why meetings must die because most meetings are ineffective and drag on far too long.

Meetings have become such drudgery, such annoying nuisances and distractions to our day.

We go into a meeting, and we sit for thirty minutes to an hour. Things get discussed, but nothing really important, and a lot of times, most of the people in the room don't have to be there for the meeting. These people are disengaged and burning the organization's money.

Think about this:

If you have ten people in your meeting, with each person making an average of twenty dollars per hour, and the meeting lasts an hour. This equals $200 for the meeting.

Now imagine there are ten meetings like this.

The organization just spent $2,000!

Not only are meetings taking up the time of your team members, meetings are burning through the cash in your bank account.

This means you need to hook the attendees of the meetings held. How do you do this? What can you do to make sure that they're interested, engaged, and ready to hear the message of the meeting?

This is where your hook comes into play.

You've got to create a clear and compelling idea. This idea grabs the attention of those attending the meeting. You have to plan to deliver something of meaning. You must help your people understand the meeting is important and you have a reason for calling the meeting.

When you're able to hook your team members, meetings no longer need to die. They move into the land of productivity.

Lead the meeting with the most interesting thing the attendees will get out of the meeting. Make them see what is coming and how they all play a greater part in the grand story.

When you open your meeting with something exciting, you are hooking your audience.

## YOUR CUSTOMERS

The third audience in need of a hook is that of your customers. You're leading this organization providing value to your customers.

But how do your customers know what you're offering?

You've got to hook them.

Why does the customer need to do business with you? What drives them to be in business? Find this reason. Now you know why they're doing what they do. This means you can now tailor the pitch (and hook) to the specific customer. You will make them feel special. They will feel you get them. They will be hooked.

**

Overall, we just have to make sure we're hooking our audiences whether they're our team members, the people we have in a meeting, or the customers we're trying to win over.

I believe it doesn't take very much to hook the people with whom you're interacting.

What would it take to craft a great hook and pull people into your organization? Begin hooking your audiences and you may see some exponential growth in your business and relationships.

## DISCUSSION QUESTIONS:

1. How are you hooking your audience? Do you think they're paying attention?
2. What needs to change about your hook? What could you do better?
3. Who is your audience?
4. How has your company wasted time on meetings? What do you need to do to change this?

## SCENE 8:

# OVERCOMING FEAR

---

*"Nobody is gonna hit as hard as life, but it ain't how hard you can hit. It's how hard you can get hit and keep moving forward. It's how much you can take and keep moving forward. That's how winning is done."*

—ROCKY BALBOA

Marty Himmel has been a lot of things. He has been a dental technician. He has been an assistant pastor. Now, Marty is a web developer creating websites that help people.

In 2020, Marty found himself in an interesting position. Within the first week of the year, Marty realized he had watched a movie a day.

Then he had a thought.

What if he could watch a movie every day of the year? This would total 366 days since it was a leap year the year he attempted this feat.

He decided to challenge himself and make this a reality. He would watch at least one movie every day.

He knew this wouldn't be easy. It would be something that would stretch his bandwidth.

During the year, he faced adversity in completing his challenge due to house projects, work, and other commitments. His challenge even made him have a few sleepless nights!

By the end of 2020, Marty was able to say he accomplished his goal. He watched 366 movies.

Watching that many movies, you would think a lot of duds were in the bunch. Surprisingly, he found most of the movies enjoyable. Maybe 5–10 percent of the movies were bad.

There was only one movie he didn't finish watching.

I was able to sit down with Marty over a cup of coffee at our local coffee shop, Aldea Coffee. When I asked what his favorite movies are, Marty had two that sprung to mind. He really enjoys watching *Braveheart*. The other movie is a series, *The Lord of the Rings* trilogy, which is a must-watch movie series, he says.

When talking about leadership lessons and movies, Marty chose to dive into *Braveheart*. The movie is near and dear to his heart. The scene he remembers most vividly goes something like this:

"There's a point in the movie where they're all painted up and they're getting ready to storm across the fields. Everybody's kind of fearful of that. William Wallace gets out there, and he's riding across and talking about how they may not make it through this day. They may not make it home to their families, but they're going to give the enemy a fight they can't forget."

That scene in *Braveheart* inspired Marty. He saw that despite the fear and the losses that were going to come that day, the characters were going to fight. This led to the leadership lesson he saw in *Braveheart*.

Whatever you're facing, whatever battle is in front of you, you still need to face those fears and fight the fight that needs to be fought.

When asked how he has applied this in his leadership, he had a great answer. Marty has had huge transitions in his career, from dental technician to assistant pastor to web developer. Each transition was different. Each job offered new challenges that required skills not directly related to his previous job. His mind began to fill with doubts. Would he have the skills to do the work he was going into? He held onto a bit of fear as he made these transitions. The fear of not being able to accomplish what came next created doubt and a lack of confidence.

When he received a phone call with a potential employer, the employer gave him a challenge. He was told if he could do a little project, the employer would give him a job. This was an opportunity for Marty to face the fear in front of him. He could practice the lesson of bravery he had seen in *Braveheart*.

Challenge on! It was time to step onto the battlefield, face fear, and give it his all.

Turning in his project, he wasn't sure if the work he had done was what they wanted. He later found out it was. He landed the job.

By getting over the fear he was facing, he was able to move forward and change his career field.

## IT'S TIME FOR YOU TO OVERCOME FEAR

Leadership is scary. We know that when we step into a new leadership position. We don't know what's ahead of us.

It's kind of like the movie *Scream*.

*Scream* is a horror movie about a killer named Ghostface. In horror movies, the bad guy is always hiding just around the corner. You never know where he's going to pop out from.

He could be hidden in the dark corner where the light fails to shine. He could be hiding underneath the bed, or he might be in the dimly lit basement to which you failed to bring a flashlight. You just never know where the villain will be next.

It's this sense of the unknown that keeps horror movie watchers on their toes. They know something is going to come. It will probably be scary. They're ready for the freak out, though.

It's what they enjoy watching and participating in. They're ready to face their fears.

Leadership is a lot like that. We don't know what's coming. We can't predict the future. We don't know where the next struggle will be. And that is scary. It can create fear in us because we don't know what's going to happen next.

Leaders must face the unknown. We have to face the scary situations that will pop up from the shadows. There's no way around this. That's what leaders do. They lead into the unknown, even if there isn't full confidence they will come out on the other side.

That's one of the awesome things about movies. Movies show us multiple different ways to face fear and overcome the doubts and fears we have.

> We don't know what's coming. We can't predict the future. We don't know where the next struggle will be. And that is scary.

We can be scared, we can know there will be challenges, we can also move forward knowing we have done what is right. By leading the charge, as William Wallace—Mel Gibson's character in *Braveheart*—did, we can mount the metaphorical horse and storm the gates of fear.

This isn't some wishy-washy idea. Leaders face their fears every day.

Every time I get up to present a message to students in our youth group, I have to overcome my fear. I have to tell myself that a failure here won't result in my death. Rather, I must remind myself the words I'm going to share will encourage the students to whom I am speaking. The students will have a chance to hear a life-giving message. This gives me a reason to overcome my fear.

I'm not the only leader who has to overcome fear. History is full of leaders, in real life and from movies, who have overcome fear. Take a look at the following leaders.

**ROBERT PATTINSON:**
Robert Pattinson, a professional actor, was interviewed for the Willie Geist *Sunday Sitdown*. Pattinson was raw with the audience. He opened up about the fear and anxiety he felt as he auditioned for roles.

Even though he acts before the camera for his job, he would fear auditions.

Pattinson said, "I used to get so paralyzed with anxiety before auditions; I just couldn't do anything."

The fear he had was crippling. He was there to land the job, and all he could do was stand there. This could have been a situation Pattinson repeated over and over again.

Yet Pattinson was able to overcome his fear. How did he do it?

He used the fear he felt to charge himself up for the audition.

During the interview, Pattinson said, "The only thing that ever worked is just to use that anxiety as a charge. You build everything from anxiety and fear."

He found a way to use what could have held him back, and instead, he used it to make himself a better actor.

### RICHARD BRANSON:

It's hard to imagine Sir Richard Branson, founder of the myriad Virgin companies, fearing anything. Branson is known for his love of doing extreme things in life and in business. Branson has launched multiple businesses, all of them very different. He launched Virgin Records, moved into the airline business with Virgin Airlines because he was unhappy with the way airlines were being run, and wound up founding Virgin Galactic, an American spaceflight company looking to bring consumers to space.

What does Sir Richard Branson fear?

Branson fears *public speaking*. That's right, the man who has launched many successful companies can be afraid of speaking to crowds of people.

I love this. It makes him relatable because he has the same fear as 75 percent of the general public.

Branson has shared multiple ways he has overcome fear. I have chosen two of his methods for overcoming fear to share with you.

The first way Branson overcomes fear is to imagine himself in a situation where he is comfortable. In an interview for *Entrepreneur.com*, Branson told the magazine:

*"When you need to speak in front of a crowd, close your mind to the fact that you're on a stage with hundreds of people watching you, and instead imagine yourself in a situation where you'd be comfortable speaking to a group."*

Basically, he stops thinking about where he is. Branson finds a place in his mind where he is comfortable.

Then, he imagines himself being there. This helps alleviate the fears Branson has of public speaking.

There's another trick Branson uses to overcome his fear. He uses a method proclaimed by Winston Churchill (remember his story in *The Darkest Hour*?).

Branson says:

"Like Churchill, I found that if you practice, practice, practice, then practice some more, that will gradually mitigate the fear of public speaking, no matter how debilitating. Repeat the speech until you are even hearing the phrases in your dreams, and it will be much easier to deliver."

If you want to overcome fear, you can do what Winston Churchill and Richard Branson do. You can practice, practice, practice. The more you practice, the more comfortable you will become.

I think back to when I first began giving presentations. I, too, suffer from the fear of public speaking. My speeches would be filled with umms, ahhs, and ya knows. They were sloppy. That was until I began to practice. I joined a local Toastmasters club. There, I could practice the art of public speaking with less fear than if I were to present in front of a paying audience. Through repetition, I've become a much better public speaker. The fear of being in front of an audience has diminished considerably.

Repetition works to remove fear.

**LAURA WALKER LEE:**
Laura Walker Lee is the CEO of AG Capital. AG Capital is a fund that focuses on the advancement of culture by way of world-class creators, impactful storytelling, and unique live events. Founded in 2015, AG Capital has produced and/or financed projects for Will Smith and Westbrook, Brad Pitt and Plan B, Ava DuVernay, Rob Siegel, and Beau Willimon, among others.

She learned to overcome the fear of reaching out to others by adopting the mantra, "Courage is fear hanging on for a minute longer."

This is what she had to say about overcoming fear:

"Of all the responsibilities I have as a CEO, the one that can be intimidating is reaching out to creatives and luminaries that I admire, which is essential to the growth of my business. I overcame this fear by adopting the mantra, 'Courage is fear hanging on for a minute longer,' which is a quote by General George S. Patton that was first taught to me by my father who was in the Navy. This simple but powerful phrase has always helped me convert nervousness into action, and those actions have helped me reach my goals throughout my career."

Lee faced the fear of reaching out to people she admired. Many people have this fear. It is scary to reach out to people we look up to. We doubt that the people we admire will have time to answer our questions. We may feel we aren't worthy of being talked to by these successful people. Lee discovered this isn't true.

The way Lee overcame fear reminded me of a great movie based on the true story of Benjamin Mee, *We Bought a Zoo*.

*We Bought a Zoo* stars Mark Wahlberg as single father Benjamin Mee. Mee lost his wife, and he wants to start his life over. He buys a large house with a zoo on the property. His daughter is excited about the zoo. His son is not thrilled.

In the movie, Mee says:

*"You know, sometimes all you need is twenty seconds of insane courage. Just literally twenty seconds of just embarrassing bravery. And I promise you, something great will come of it."*

Mee took a chance in buying the house. He took a chance in keeping the zoo running. He had to overcome the fear of failure. He did this through taking twenty seconds to do something scary. When he got through those seemingly long twenty seconds, he discovered he didn't die. He then repeated the process over and over again.

You can adopt Mee's way of overcoming fear. Whenever you face fear, take twenty seconds to stare fear in the face. You do this by taking action for twenty seconds. Then another twenty. And then another. By breaking it down to twenty seconds of action, you can get through any fear.

**

Fear can be crippling. It can destroy your authority as a leader. However, if you adopt the methods of the three leaders above, especially Mee's use of the twenty seconds of insane courage from *We Bought a Zoo*, you will have a great way to overcome fear.

## DISCUSSION QUESTIONS:

1. How has fear stopped you from pursuing a leadership position or initiative?
2. Could you implement your own version of Mee's twenty seconds of insane courage? What would this look like for you?
3. What's your biggest fear?
4. Do you feel like you're alone in your fear? Who could you partner with to walk through it?

# SCENE 9:

# MASTER YOURSELF

---

*"Tonight you have learned the final and greatest truth of the ninja: that ultimate mastering comes not from the body, but from the mind. Together, there is nothing your four minds cannot accomplish."*

—MASTER SPLINTER, *TEENAGE MUTANT NINJA TURTLES*

Skip Prichard is a longtime friend and fellow blogger. He runs the successful blog "Skip Prichard: Leadership Insights." His site also hosts the podcast *Aim Higher* where he and his coworkers discuss how to take your leadership to the next level. He is an Inc. Top 100 Leadership Speaker and author of the Wall Street Journal best-selling book *The Book of Mistakes: 9 Secrets to Creating a Successful Future.*

In his book, Skip uses a fictional tale (sound familiar?) to help us understand nine mistakes to avoid if we want a successful future. These are all mistakes he's experienced or seen others experience. When we become aware of damaging mistakes, we're better able to avoid them.

In an interview I conducted with Skip, he shared his thoughts on movies and how they can make us better leaders. Skip said that everything we read and watch influences us beyond what we may realize. Even our friends have extraordinary influence over us, so who we are around is a critical success factor.

Skip said he is constantly watching movies and learning lessons from them.

Skip pulled leadership ideas from multiple movies.

In a previous interview I conducted with him for my blog, Skip shared a line from the Jack Nicholson movie *As Good as It Gets*. Nicholson's character says, "You make me want to be a better man." Skip equated this to wanting to be a leader who inspires others to be better.

He's used the movie *Elf* to explore leadership. One of the lessons he pulled from *Elf* was that pure joy will win over even the most resistant.

He has also shared about *Star Wars* in his blog. The leadership lesson he shared from *Star Wars* that really stuck out to me was this one: Mastering self is the beginning of the leadership journey. Leading requires us to work on ourselves before we can work on others. If we're not in a good position mentally, physically, and emotionally, it will be hard to lead others.

Skip continued by saying movies and fiction allow us to learn from others without direct experience. Movies and fiction can teach us empathy. We get a small taste of what it's like to be in another's shoes. These outlets are not merely entertainment. They can transform us through the power of the story, and that transformation can impact not only one person, but also a community, and even the world.

## "I'm constantly watching movies and learning lessons from them."

—SKIP PRICHARD

Skip's comments made me think about something many people overlook when it comes to leadership. Leadership is about leading others. It's such a simple concept that it often gets overlooked. We cannot overlook this basic concept of leadership. More importantly, leadership is about leading yourself well first. We must learn how to master our self. Without self-mastery, you will have a difficult time leading others.

Merriam-Webster provides a great definition of self-mastery:

*Self-mastery is the ability to control one's own desires or impulses.*

This definition brings me back to an experience I had working in a manufacturing facility. The shipping manager had shipped an order to a customer. The customer complained they never received the shipment. Our shipping manager swore he shipped it to them. He even had documentation from the shipping company.

What happened next showed a lack of self-mastery by the owner of the company. It also was a deciding factor in why I left the organization.

The owner began questioning the shipping manager. He wouldn't believe the shipping documentation, the information in the system, or the shipping manager. His voice began to rise. You could hear the berating throughout the office area. Not only did he berate him in the office, but he also followed the shipping manager out of his office, down the hallway, and out to the production floor, all while yelling, screaming, and cursing at him.

It was ugly. It was also a display of the lack of self-mastery the owner of the company had over himself. He let anger and frustration boil over the top and spill out into the office.

What would someone who had self-mastery do?

He wouldn't have responded in the manner the owner of this company did. Instead, he would take steps to calm himself. He would lead himself.

This could mean using a measured breathing exercise to calm down. It may mean counting to ten before reacting.

When it came time to act, a self-mastered leader would then calmly talk to the employee.

A self-mastered leader would ask questions, get details, and then figure out the next moves to make.

A self-mastered leader would not blow up at the employee.

A self-mastered leader would gather all the information so he didn't react poorly.

*Self-mastery is the ability to control one's own desires or impulses.*

## WHY SELF-MASTERY MATTERS

The above example discouraged my coworkers in the office. They saw a horrible display of leadership from the person steering the ship. If he could do this to our shipping manager, who was next on his list?

Leaders have to be willing to control their impulses. They cannot act on their first thought or inclination. Doing so can damage their reputation. It can damage their respect. It can, and will, drive your best people away.

I've seen people leave organizations because of this. I've left organizations because of this. They get tired of random outbursts, uncontrolled expletive-laden tirades, and being treated poorly. When leaders cannot control themselves, people leave.

This isn't the only reason to learn to master yourself. Self-mastery isn't strictly about your emotions. Self-mastery goes deeper. It cuts to the core of who you are and what you can do. When you learn to master yourself, you learn to take yourself to a higher level.

In the business world, you're going to lead people you do not like. These people will rub you the wrong way. This annoyance comes from nothing other than their presence. They have done nothing wrong, but for some reason they bother you.

A leader who doesn't have self-mastery would quickly get rid of the employee who annoys them. They don't want to be bothered by someone like that. So, they let them go.

What happens when they're annoyed the next time? They decide to let that person go as well. Soon, all that remains for the leader is a shell of an organization with no one left. If employees are left, they have no trust in the leader.

This is why self-mastery matters. It is one of the core principles of leadership.

## HOW TO MASTER YOURSELF

When I think of self-mastery, my mind wanders to the exploits seen in the 1984 film *The Karate Kid*.

*The Karate Kid* tells the story of young Daniel LaRusso. He is the main protagonist in *The Karate Kid* and many of its sequels.

Daniel's fellow high school students bullied him. Because of the bullying, Mr. Miyagi steps in and intervenes in the conflict between Daniel-San and his rival Johnny Lawrence.

Mr. Miyagi becomes Daniel's sensei. He agrees to teach Daniel the ways of karate. The way Mr. Miyagi teaches Daniel karate is unorthodox. He has Daniel master common motions through everyday chores.

Mr. Miyagi has Daniel paint a fence with up-and-down motions. Next, he has Daniel wax on, wax off his car. Circular motions with his hands. All of this seems pointless.

Why does Mr. Miyagi have Daniel do these repetitive motions? These motions, these tasks were to help Daniel learn to master the motions of his body.

Daniel eventually pushes back against Mr. Miyagi's training methods. Tired of doing these "chores" for his sensei, Daniel wants to be *taught* the art of karate. This is when Mr. Miyagi shows Daniel that all the work he has done was honing his mastery of karate. Daniel was able to move about and defend himself with the repetitive motions he mastered from the tasks Mr. Miyagi set out before him.

Daniel eventually got to take on Johnny at the All-Valley Karate Tournament. In a match prior to the final, one of Cobra Kai's fighters is encouraged to do an illegal move on Daniel. The Cobra Kai sensei, John Kreese, tells Bobby to put Daniel out of commission. He wanted Bobby to do whatever it took to break Daniel. Bobby does an illegal kick to Daniel's knee and almost makes Daniel exit the tournament. Everyone believes Daniel should quit. It was too dangerous for him to continue. Daniel chooses to have Mr. Miyagi give him a pain suppression massage to numb the pain. Mr. Miyagi agrees and performs the massage. Daniel is able to get back into the ring in time to fight Johnny.

Daniel and Johnny begin their battle. Daniel wins the first two rounds. Johnny sees an opportunity and attacks Daniel's weak leg. Daniel is in excruciating pain. He cannot stand on the injured leg. He transitions to the crane technique position. The referee signals the next bout is ready to be fought. Daniel pushes off on his good leg and lands a kick to Johnny's face, winning the All-Valley Karate Tournament.

Daniel had mastered his body and the pain he felt.

As we begin to master ourselves, we may feel like Daniel. We feel that the motions we're going through are repetitive, unimportant, even lazy. They feel like we're never going to get to the point of mastery. It is when we get to this point, we are often at the point of mastery. So, what does it take to master yourself? It takes:

**REPETITIVE TASKS:**
When we first enter a leadership position, we may not be given mission-critical tasks to accomplish. Instead, we're given tasks that seem mundane.

- We have to prepare a report to be given weekly to the board of directors.
- We may be told to observe the work of a production worker and report what we saw the employee do.

These tasks seem repetitive. They may even seem below us as leaders. Yet these repetitive tasks are building us up as leaders.

Let's break down the two scenarios I gave above.

The weekly report you gave to the board of directors was repetitive. You felt like you were giving the same report over and over again. You are. However, the report was doing something for you. By repeating the report week after week, the mission of the organization was driven into your psyche. You drilled into yourself the *why* of the organization. You can now repeat it verbatim.

What about watching the production worker do his task again and again? This wasn't so you could spy on him or figure out what he was doing wrong. Instead, you began to see the employee as a person. You got to know him better. You learned his story because while you were observing him, you were also talking to him. You learned how to master the art of conversation with someone you lead. Another thing that happens as you spend time with the employee is that you become a better leader. Not only is the employee learning, but you're also learning as well. Your regular repeated tasks are similar to the tasks Mr. Miyagi had Daniel do in *The Karate Kid*.

**PUSH THROUGH THE PAIN:**
Daniel had to conquer the pain he felt after the ruthless attack by the Cobra Kai team member. He couldn't let the pain stop him. You can't either.

Leaders will face pain throughout their time in these supervisory positions. From betrayals to the loss of great employees, leaders hurt. They have the battle wounds of leadership.

This pain can be overwhelming. You may believe you don't have anything left to give. Let me tell you: **YOU DO.**

There is always a little more in the tank. You can always push through the pain for another minute or two. You can get to the end if you are willing to go through the hurt.

When you come out on the other side, you will still hurt. However, you will also know you did exactly what you needed to do. You fought hard. You did what was right. You led well.

**FINDING AND BECOMING A MASTER:**
Self-mastery isn't easy. It comes through a lot of work. You have to do repetitive, boring tasks until you learn from them. And you have to push through the pain you feel.

Sometimes it's best if you find a master who is willing to teach you. Daniel found himself a master in Mr. Miyagi. Mr. Miyagi took Daniel under his wing and showed him how to become a karate master. What would happen if you found a master to help mold you?

Finding a master isn't as difficult as you may think it is. Masters often show up at just the right time.

I've found masters in multiple areas of my life. For public speaking, Jerry Conrad was the master I looked up to. He was the president of our local Toastmasters club. He helped guide me on my way to mastering my public speaking skills.

In youth ministry, Pastor Rick South was a master. He was my youth pastor for my entire middle and high school years. He poured leadership skills into me as he allowed me to take on additional roles of responsibilities.

Masters are all around us. We only have to look for them and they will appear.

Daniel had Mr. Miyagi. I had Rick South.

Who will your leadership master be?

You, too, could become a leadership master. When you do these things, you may even become a master of yourself. We saw Daniel become a karate master and eventually lead his own dojo. What will you accomplish through mastering yourself?

## DISCUSSION QUESTIONS:

1. Have you mastered yourself? Why do you feel this way?
2. What do you need to do to better master yourself?
3. Can you implement mundane tasks into your routine to help you gain a skill?
4. What happens when you feel pain or pressure? How do you push through this feeling?

# SCENE 10:

# FINDING A MENTOR

——

*"When an individual acquires great power, the use or misuse of that power is everything. Will it be used for the greater good? Or will it be used for personal or for destructive ends? Now this is a question we must all ask ourselves. Why? Because we are mutants."*

—PROFESSOR X, *X-MEN: THE LAST STAND*

What would Batman do in this situation?

That's not a question you hear every day in leadership training for business executives.

David Kahn has been a teacher for twenty-five years. During these years, Kahn found himself giving the same presentation repeatedly. There was nothing mind-blowing about the leadership content he was sharing. In fact, he found repeating the standard thoughts on leadership boring. There was nothing unique or challenging about the content he was presenting. It felt like everyone else's thoughts.

During one presentation, things changed. He began to free-wheel the presentation. This led him to ask the business executives a strange question.

He posed a situation and asked, "What would Batman do in this situation?"

The room grew eerily quiet.

Then an executive in the back laughed and gave Kahn an example of what Batman would do.

This changed the trajectory of how Kahn taught and was the impetus for his book *Cape, Spandex, Briefcase: Leadership Lessons from Superheroes.*

Kahn has gone on to give his old presentations with a new twist. No longer are they dry and boring with examples from Jack Welch or other classic business leaders. Kahn now uses examples from comic books to teach the principles of leadership (sound familiar?).

In my interview with Kahn, he said, "In the last twenty years, we, as a society, have taken superheroes a little more seriously than we used to. They used to be a joke and now they're the biggest movies in the world. They're the biggest TV shows. Superheroes are everywhere and they're being treated in a serious way."

This is great news for the *reel leader.*

# "What would Batman do in this situation?"

—DAVID KAHN

The way we learn and interact with the entertainment around us is changing. People are learning how to use comic books, video games (just ask Jon D. Harrison about leadership and video games), and even movies to help them become better leaders.

Kahn also said, "As a generation, that's something we can now relate to. This can be a more serious topic. In my book, I use this example: The chance of me sitting down and having lunch with Jack Welch or Michael Jordan is about the same as me sitting down having lunch with Peter Parker (Spider-Man). It's not going to happen. Whether they're fictional or not fictional, they're so out of the grasp of my reality in the world that the lessons you can learn from both are the same because they're all mythical figures."

Think about that for a minute. Kahn compared Jack Welch (former chairman and CEO of General Electric), Michael Jordan (former professional basketball player, most notably for the Chicago Bulls, and movie star), and Peter Parker to the same type of character: *MYTHICAL*. They're out of the common leader's reach to ever form a one-on-one relationship with.

There's a good chance you'll never sit down and have dinner with Jack Welch or Michael Jordan. There's no way you're going to sit down with Peter Parker. Yet... this doesn't diminish the lessons we can learn from Jack Welch, Michael Jordan, or Peter Parker's stories.

## FINDING A MENTOR

Every leader needs to think about finding a mentor. Many leaders struggle to find a mentor because they believe their mentor has to be an in-person, in-their-face mentor. They fail to see the mentors they can find through the silver screen.

Movies are full of mentors to look up to. Kahn shared how Peter Parker could be your mentor, if you let him.

Examining Peter Parker's life, you see how he has taken on Uncle Ben's advice, "With great power comes great responsibility." He lives out what he was taught. He continues to teach us what he's learned. He's fictional but just as relatable as someone like Jack Welch, Michael Hyatt (former president and COO of Thomas Nelson Publishing), or Dan Pink (former host and co-executive producer of *Crowd Control*, a television series about human behavior).

Welch, Hyatt, and Pink share their wisdom through their books and blogs. They've been my mentors many times over. I am grateful for their willingness to pour into people they have never met. I have grown leaps and bounds because of the work of men like these.

For example, I began my blogging journey because of two remote mentors. Dan Miller, author of *48 Days to the Work You Love,* and Michael Hyatt, author of *Platform*. These men helped me understand the potential I had within me. They helped me understand the importance of building a platform to share the message within me. Without these two remote mentors, I wouldn't have written this book. I wouldn't have taken the steps to improve my thoughts and soundtracks, as author Jon Acuff would say. I would have kept doing the things I had been doing.

Instead, I found myself writing a blog about leadership. I wrote about things such as how to become more productive, what leadership looks like, and how to use movies to lead better. My blog led me to be labeled as one of the top fifty leadership bloggers in the world.

That's the power of a mentor.

But what if you can't relate to a Hyatt, Miller, or Welch? What do you do then?

You find a mentor where you can. I want to recommend you check out your local movie theater or Netflix to find yours.

I haven't always learned from the names above. I've also learned from great movie characters. You can too. Let's look at a few movie mentors I've had.

## PETER PARKER/SPIDER-MAN

When Peter Parker first gained his powers in *Spider-Man*, he became a wrestler. He saw an ad looking for wrestlers. He thought this would be a great idea with the power he'd recently gained. At his first wrestling match, the owner of the wrestling organization is robbed. The robber runs past

Parker, and he shrugs his shoulders and lets the robber go. That's a major failure on Parker's part that ended in the murder of his Uncle Ben.

Or, when Parker is learning to travel using his web shooters. He's not naturally skilled or talented. He struggles to control his direction, speed, and power. He had to practice over and over again until he got the hang of it. After much practice, Parker is able to swing, almost effortlessly, around New York City.

What did I learn from Peter Parker? His mentoring taught me a few things. The first is not to ignore people in trouble, even if they're jerks. You see trouble, you act. If you don't, you may learn the greatest leadership lesson of all time: With great power comes great responsibility.

The second lesson he taught me was to keep trying. I mentioned earlier Peter Parker struggled to web sling. I struggle to do a lot of the things I first set out to do. I have to continually practice, like Peter Parker did. As I practice, I gain competence in the skills I'm working on. The longer I do it, the better I get. While I'll never shoot webs and swing on webbing over the cityscape of New York City, though I felt like it during an ice climbing trip, I can improve my skills through practice. So can you.

**GANDALF**

Gandalf is the wise wizard in the *Lord of the Rings* trilogy. We see him leading and guiding little Frodo through all three movies. His presence was consistent throughout.

His mentoring presence was always there, though many times unseen.

The wisdom he dispenses to Frodo is invaluable. So much so that we, in the real world, would be wise to heed his advice. In this way, Gandalf became a movie mentor.

What are some of the ways he mentored me? Gandalf mentored me through the following quotes:

*"So do all who live to see such times. But that is not for them to decide. All we have to decide is what to do with the time that is given to us. There are other forces at work in this world, Frodo, besides the will of evil. Bilbo was meant to find the Ring. In which case, you were also meant to have it. And that is an encouraging thought."*

Frodo had just mentioned he wished the ring had never come to him. He wanted none of what had happened to have happened. Gandalf, the wise wizard he is, tells Frodo that no one wishes for the trials and tribulations of life. They don't want to do the hard things. Yet we cannot avoid the challenges. In fact, we should be encouraged that the trials chose us. That means there is hope, and we can make a difference in the world.

I love remembering this. It helps remind me that I can get through the difficult times of leadership. Bumps in the road aren't going to derail me. They're not going to derail you either. We need to keep pressing forward. We have to choose what to do with what we're given.

*"Farewell... my brave hobbits. My work is now finished. Here at last, on the shores of the sea... comes the end of our Fellowship. I will not say do not weep... not all tears are an evil."*

In this quote from *Lord of the Rings: The Return of the King,* Gandalf realizes his time with the Hobbits is ending. Gandalf has completed the work he had set out to do. Now it was time for Gandalf to depart from those he helped with the mission of the Ring.

This taught me that our times as leaders must come to an end at some point. We have to figure out why we're a leader and what our mission is. When we've accomplished that mission, it may be time to move on to another role or organization. We're not meant to stay in one place forever.

With *The Lord of the Rings,* we're able to have Gandalf as a mentor for multiple outings. He was in all three films. He was also in the extended editions. This means we interacted with the tale of Gandalf for over nine hours. That's a lot of time to be mentored by Gandalf.

### TONY STARK

Tony Stark was the character hero *Iron Man.* He starred in multiple *Iron Man* movies along with *The Avengers, Spider-Man: Homecoming,* and other films. He was a hard-working, stoic man. He had his faults. He also had times where he could be seen as a great on-screen mentor.

In *Captain America: Civil War,* Tony Stark mentored us in the use of grace. Bucky Barnes/The Winter Soldier was

Steve Rogers/Captain America's original partner. Bucky was believed dead, but he had been turned into a secret weapon named The Winter Soldier. As The Winter Soldier, he killed Tony Stark's parents.

Imagine the rage boiling up in Tony Stark when he learns what really happened to his parents. However, instead of killing Bucky, Tony chooses grace. He lets Bucky live. He even works next to him in future movies.

This is grace in action. This is something leaders need to learn when dealing with people. Our people are going to make mistakes. Can we extend grace to them?

Tony Stark also mentored us in how to be a sacrificial leader. In *Avengers: Endgame,* Tony knew what would happen when he donned the Infinity Gauntlet and snapped his fingers. Sure, he would set everything back to the way it should be. Yet, Tony knew the power released from the snap would kill him. Knowing this didn't stop Tony from doing what he knew he had to do. He had to sacrifice his life for the life of everyone else. He showed us how to be sacrificial and think of others.

**

Don't be afraid to look at movies for leadership mentors. They are there. They're more relatable than many real-life business leaders.

Go watch a movie and see how the main character can be a mentor to you. You'll get some one-on-one mentoring time with them. You'll be able to spend more time with your fictional mentors than you will with those in real-life.

Their stories are told, faults and all, so you can see they're just like you, but maybe with a little superpower thrown in.

They're there, ready to mentor you.

They're just waiting for you to hit the play button.

## DISCUSSION QUESTIONS:

1. Do you have a mentor? Why or why not?
2. What can you do to find a mentor today?
3. How could finding a mentor change your life?
4. Do you think fictional mentors can be of value to you?

## SCENE 11:

# MANAGING EFFECTIVELY

———

*"Just because someone stumbles and loses their path, doesn't mean they're lost forever."*
—CHARLES XAVIER, *X-MEN: DAYS OF FUTURE PAST*

To many leaders, the thought of managing goes against the grain of what they believe leadership is.

In a *Harvard Business Review* article, Vineet Nayar states three distinct differences exist between managers and leaders. They are:

1. Counting value vs. creating value.
2. Having circles of influence vs. circles of power.
3. Leading people vs. managing work.

It seems that leading and managing are two distinct arenas. However, there are times leading and managing intersect.

David Hayter is a man of many roles. One of his most famous roles is as the voice of Solid Snake in the *Metal Gear Solid* video game series. He voiced the main character of the video game you played. But Hayter is more than that. I discovered this when I researched him for this book.

Hayter is also a voice-actor (he voiced King Shark in *The Flash* TV series), producer, director, and writer in the film industry. There are two movies you will definitely know his work from: *X-Men* and *X2: X-Men United*. He also wrote the screenplays for *The Scorpion King*, the Netflix series *Warrior Nun*, and other entertainment properties.

In my interview with Hayter, we discussed the difficult challenge of managing your team. Hayter had two differing ideas about this aspect of leadership. The ideas seem to be contradictory, yet I think they can both be done effectively. You do have to be aware of how your team will respond to each style of communication. When managing a team, you may have the cool and collected style of managing or you may have a more hard-nosed stance. What do those varying types of leadership look like? They could be:

You have this grand vision for what you want your organization to accomplish. You've put everything together in your mind. It looks grand. You've figured out how all the pieces of the puzzle fit together. Then, a team member steps into the picture. They do something you did not expect.

CUT!

This doesn't fit with what you had in mind for your organization. The team member's action has ruined your whole plan. Or so you think when you allow your mind to jump there. Hayter said most of the time people jump to this conclusion.

They ask what the heck did that person just do? Why did they do that? It's not the way I would do it. It's not the way I planned it out. You didn't read my mind.

Instead of jumping to these types of conclusions, the cool and collected leader does something different.

Hayter then shared about his experience working with Paul Greengrass. Greengrass was the director for *United 93*, *Captain Phillips* (starring Tom Hanks), and other amazing movies. This director has success behind his belt. He knows how to make a great film.

The experience Hayter had with Greengrass was different from most directors. Greengrass didn't yell and scream at the actors. He, instead, was super nice and respectful. This doesn't mean Greengrass was a pushover. No, Greengrass knew what he wanted. He was, as Hayter put it, *exacting.*

Greengrass would come in and respectfully say, "You know, look... I know, I know you've gone through this eight different times. It's still not working for me. I think we need to go in a whole new direction."

The way Greengrass did this wouldn't break the person being talked to. The overwhelming nature of the project wouldn't spill over into the way he treated people on set.

Hayter then shared a similar experience with his time working with director Ang Lee. Lee has directed multiple great movies. Many of the titles you may know. Lee's work includes

*Crouching Tiger, Hidden Dragon, Hulk, Life of Pi, Gemini Man,* and many other titles. Many moviegoers know his work.

When Lee worked with those on set, he was kind, gentle, and caring. He rarely was rude. But there were times when directors like Lee and Greengrass had to get down to brass tacks. It wasn't all sunshine and roses. When it came down to the wire, they began to communicate in a more serious manner. They would clearly state the reasoning behind a rush. Maybe they needed a helmet painted in the next half hour or else it would cost them an additional quarter million dollars in shooting. There were times these directors had to take a tough stance.

But how do you lead sternly while being gentle?

Hayter gave me a couple of steps to help make sure you get things done while being kind. The first thing Hayter does is to tell the team what you're trying to set up. In the movie world, it's called "story beats." These "story beats" help set the scene, pace, etc. for the movie.

The "story beats" Hayter tries to convey are the moments when a character discovers something major, a big idea, and how to tie things together. This gets the actor thinking about where they're going rather than just the moment they're in. By helping your team understand what is being set up, you help them see the reason behind their work. It helps them see the bigger picture, which is difficult when they don't know the reasoning behind their work. It helps them to see where their work is leading them.

Isn't that cool?

For leaders who want to feel fresh or spontaneous, Hayter gives this additional piece of advice. In the movie world, the director says to the actor, "Okay, I want you to discover this line. The line is. 'Where's the key? Oh, it's over there.'" The actor repeats the line, and the director has to tell the actor, "No, that's not how you say it. *Discover* the line." They help the actor discover the tone and inflection points in the line. It's not just a simple phrase.

We can use this advice to help our team understand how they come to work. It's not just a job. Their work has meaning. They need to discover the voice of their work. Instead of coming in moping and dreary, come to the office full of excitement. Then, you bring a new kind of energy to the workplace. Help them discover how to come to work this way. It brings enthusiasm and energy. It changes the tone of the workplace.

The last piece of advice on this type of leadership Hayter gave was to help your team understand how our actions affect the company. Hayter has seen directors come in thinking the movie is going to make all kinds of money. That's their focus. It's not about creating anything meaningful; their focus is on making money.

When these leaders choose a different tactic, the movies become more powerful. What is this tactic? They begin telling their team, "If we do this, here's how it's going to affect the company. This is how what you do will make the team look great."

> If we do this, here's how it's going to affect the company. This is how what you do will make the team look great.

—DAVID HAYTER

Instead of focusing on the money aspect of the work, focus on the people. Help your team become personally invested in the ultimate outcome. When you help your people believe in the work, you help them create something special from it. Lean into it so that twenty years later, your people still have pride in the work they did.

## MANAGING EFFECTIVELY

We think there is a special formula to managing a team effectively. I want to tell you there's no magic wand to help you do this. Every situation will present itself differently. You will have to step back, look at the situation, and figure out what kind of management will work best.

Hayter sees this in the way movies are made. Sometimes you need to be the loving parent and gently guide the members of your team along. You help them understand that there is a reason behind all the work you're doing. When your team sees what they're working for is something special, they're willing to put more energy, effort, and time into the project.

How do you do this?

You share the vision behind the project. You help them see that the work they're doing isn't just about their wages or the company's profits.

At one of the places I've worked, we had a fantastic phrase for what we do. The phrase that helped keep everyone focused was "Enriching lives through creative furniture solutions." While this doesn't seem like much, it does help us focus on our why. We were not creating furniture just to make furniture. No, the furniture we created helped enrich the lives of the people using it. This may be through the beauty of the furniture. Or it could be through the utility of a stand-up desk, giving the user the freedom to sit or stand at any given moment throughout their workday.

When we help our team understand the positive impact their work is having, instead of the impact on the bottom line, our team will respond positively. This happens because we've given people something for which they can strive. We show them their work matters. They're not a cog in a machine turning out widget after widget. They are working for something bigger.

But Hayter also talked about another style of managing. He discussed the hard-nosed, angry leader. Is this a style of leadership that works?

He believes so. I believe so as well. However, we cannot be the hard-nosed leader all the time. It comes in fits and starts.

There has to be a reason for being hard-nosed. We may need to be hard-nosed when a deadline quickly approaches or we have a vision that needs to be communicated directly. This hard-nosed leadership style is different from the owner of the manufacturing company for whom I worked and previously mentioned. His issue came from a lack of self-mastery, not a desire to have the job done well.

Hayter shared with me an instance of the leadership with whom he worked being hard-nosed, angry, and difficult.

There is one director for whom David Hayter has worked that he found so difficult the situation terrified him. Every movie on which Hayter worked with this director, the crew said, *never again.*

It sounds like this director is a bad leader, right?

Not so, says Hayter. Despite the crew saying they will never again work for this director, they change their minds when they see the final product. The movie this director creates, along with the crew, is amazing. This causes the crew to come back again and again.

Hayter shared an experience of one crew member, Alan Cumming, who played Nightcrawler in *X-Men 2*.

Cumming said, "I will never work for this man again."

After seeing *X-Men 2*, Cumming changed his mind. Instead of fearing director Bryan Singer, Cumming was excited. He reconciled his relationship with Singer and wanted to work for him again, despite the hell he had been put through.

So, a pushy, hard-to-work-with leader can produce amazing work. They can inspire a team even if they terrify them. Once again, it's not my recommended style of leadership, but it can be effective when needed.

These moments of outbursts and frustration come not from a desire to berate and degrade your team members. They come from the desire to create something amazing.

The director Hayter mentioned did this with the movies he created. The people working for him hated the way he directed. However, they loved the outcome.

This happens often in leadership. We must crack down on bad behavior, or we quickly have to communicate the direction we're trying to go. We slip up and let our frustrations get the best of us.

This doesn't mean we're not managing effectively. It means we had moments where our management style had to change. We had to switch into a style that the people we're leading may not like. However, when we help them see the end product of what we've made together, our team often forgives a sterner style of managing.

## DISCUSSION QUESTIONS:

1. Is there a movie you can relate to this lesson? How did it change your idea of leadership?
2. What are your thoughts on leading versus managing? Are they the same or different?
3. Have you experienced a situation where you had to be a sterner leader? How did this make you feel?
4. When did you experience a difficult leader whom you discovered you actually enjoyed working with?

**SCENE 12:**

# BREAKING THE FIXED MINDSET

———

*"I'm trying to free your mind, Neo. But I can only show you the door. You're the one that has to walk through it."*

—MORPHEUS, *THE MATRIX*

We've all become trapped in a fixed mindset.

A fixed mindset is one that limits our ability to go beyond our current capabilities. One fixed mindset people hold is that they are stuck where they are. They believe they've reached the pinnacle of their career.

Think of Neo in *The Matrix*. He has a fixed mindset because he's stuck in the matrix and doesn't know there's something more for him.

We're all like Neo in one way or another.

Jon Harrison is the director of learning and organizational development at Nova Southeastern University. He helps people be more effective in their jobs and their departments. His organization provides this through training and development opportunities.

One day in 2004 or 2005, Jon sat down and joined the blogging craze happening at the time. Many people began writing blogs and sharing what they knew with the world. Jon knew he had to be one of these people and help others grow. It was in his blood.

He soon began to realize that what he was writing wasn't that different from other self-help or personal development bloggers. It all sounded the same. These bloggers were all reading the same books and giving the same summaries and applying the same ideas. It was boring. He had the same realization David Kahn did.

Jon began to look at the things he enjoyed writing about. He looked at the things that were a part of his life that he wasn't writing about but really enjoyed. He enjoyed cars, but he wasn't an expert. There was also leadership, personal development, and his career. Then something struck him. He had a hobby for over thirty years.

His hobby was playing video games.

This sparked an idea. What if video games and leadership existed on the same website? It would be unique. It would bring something new to the internet. Thus, the classically-trained.net website was born.

On his website, Jon combined his love of video games with his knowledge of leadership. His articles used the video games he had played to show how they can help you become a better leader. From there, he went on to write the book *Mastering the Game: What Video Games Can Teach Us About Success in Life.*

In my interview with Jon, he really homed in on the idea of breaking your fixed mindset. A fixed mindset is limiting. You do things to avoid growth and challenging yourself. Those with fixed mindsets will find themselves avoiding challenges, giving up early on, ignoring feedback, and feeling threatened by others. A fixed mindset is dangerous for leaders.

During our discussion, Jon homed in on one of his favorite movies. The movie is the 1999 cult classic *The Matrix*. This movie starred Keanu Reeves as Neo, Laurence Fishburne as the wise Morpheus, and Carrie-Anne Moss as Trinity. *The Matrix* made viewers question reality as the film delved into the possibility that the world may not be as it seemed. There may have been another reality out there that we didn't know.

Jon noticed a great leadership lesson in *The Matrix*. He discovered that the film really went into the idea of overcoming a fixed mindset. He said:

"In many ways, what we imagine ourselves being possible to do is what we can do. Our limits are often within ourselves. I think about the training scene with Morpheus and Neo in *The Matrix,* where he's first learning how to use these new skills he's been taught. And at one point, Morpheus asked him, 'Do you think that's air you're breathing?' This implied that what we believe to be true, the assumptions we have about the world around us, can hold us back and limit what we believe is possible, which can keep us from trying out new ideas or new things and I think that's an idea I've always taken away from that movie is, is being able to step back and question our assumptions and ask, 'Is anything I'm believing about the situation holding me back from seeing other solutions or other possibilities?'"

Jon recognized he had a fixed mindset about his career when he started his new job. He carried over fixed beliefs from his previous job that held him back. In his first year, he expected his immediate supervisor to react in the same way as his previous supervisor. He had this preconceived idea that the culture was going to be the same at his new job as it was at his old job.

> "In many ways, what we imagine ourselves being possible to do is what we can do. Our limits are often within ourselves."
>
> —JON D. HARRISON

This line of thinking held Jon back. He struggled to move past the previous nine years and step into the new culture.

About a year into his new job, he started to realize there were some definite differences. His coworkers were not out to get him. Rather, they were willing to help him. His boss was on his side. He could try new things. He could get funding for specific projects he once thought he couldn't. He wasn't used to having the level of support he was now getting. It was freeing and helped Jon break the fixed mindset he held onto for so long.

## WHAT IS YOUR FIXED MINDSET?

The role of mindset is critical for a leader. The way we think about the people we lead, those we do business with, and maybe most importantly, ourselves, can either make or break us. This is because the way we think relates to the way we act. Leading requires us to act in a confident manner. If our mindset is fixed on the negative things that could happen, we won't lead well.

Fixed mindsets typically revolve around how we view ourselves and the world around us. Our fixed mindsets tell us the world is out to get us. Or maybe our fixed mindset is telling us we're not good enough. It could also be the thought that we've reached our apex and there is no more room for growth.

These fixed mindsets will hold us back. They will keep us from stretching ourselves to the point of accomplishing something worthwhile. If we're unable to break free from our fixed mindsets, we will sit stagnant and wonder why the world keeps passing us by.

It's a dangerous trap. We have to break free from our fixed mindsets. Until we do, we will find ourselves stuck in a pattern that prohibits growth and keeps us ineffective.

## HOW TO BREAK YOUR FIXED MINDSET

Over the years, I've found myself struggling with fixed mindsets in my leadership positions and personal life. I look at myself and wonder how I was able to accomplish all that I have. It doesn't feel like I have the skills, knowledge, or capability to be here. Yet, *here I am.* I have worked on overcoming the fixed mindset into a growth mindset.

A growth mindset is a different way of thinking. We no longer believe we are not good enough. We stop believing the world is out to get us. We don't let challenges get in our way. Instead, challenges are exhilarating. We feel energized by the knowledge that we can push ourselves and grow in the areas we struggle with.

Dr. Carol Dweck has studied mindsets for years. Dr. Dweck provided this definition:

The growth mindset is based on the belief that your basic qualities are things you can cultivate through your efforts. Although people may differ in every which way in their initial talents and aptitudes, interests, or temperaments, everyone can change and grow through application and experience.

Doing this isn't as easy as taking a red pill like Neo did in *The Matrix.* We cannot simply take a magic pill or say a few magic words and change our mindset. Rather, we have to work consistently on changing our mindset from fixed to growth. We will stumble, fall, and get back up again and again when we try to break our fixed mindset. It's not easy, but it is worth it.

To break your fixed mindset, you will have to do the following:

**EMBRACE YOUR WEAKNESSES:**
Author and speaker David Rendall wrote the book *Freak Factor.* He wanted to show the world that our weaknesses are not so much weaknesses but a mirror of our strengths. We shouldn't be ashamed of our weaknesses; instead, we need to embrace them.

He uses examples from major corporations to individuals who have marketed their freak factor. One of those individuals is the German arm wrestler who had a genetic condition that made one arm larger than the other. He worked on building the muscles in this arm. In doing so, he became a global arm-wrestling sensation.

What about in the movies? I think of Ash in the movie *Evil Dead 2.*

Ash's right hand acquired an evil infection after his fight with the Deadite Linda. The hand became possessed and worked as its own independent entity. Ash couldn't have this. Finding a nearby chainsaw, Ash cut his hand off at the wrist. Many people would believe this weakness couldn't be overcome. Ash is now missing his right hand.

However, this weakness became a strength. His right hand was now unable to work against him. More importantly, Ash fashioned a harness for the chainsaw. He could now connect the chainsaw to his stump. This allowed him to use the chainsaw as part of his body.

Pretty cool, huh?

What weakness are you afraid to let the world see? This weakness may be the thing that catapults you to a growth mindset. By looking at your "weakness," you can see what makes you unique. Flip your mindset from thinking of this as a weakness to a strength.

**LEARN SLOWLY:**

Before becoming a master Jedi, Luke Skywalker had to train with Master Yoda in *Star Wars*. Luke's training was a long process. He became frustrated regularly, but he experienced growth through slow learning. Eventually, Luke became the Jedi master we know and love today.

Learning and growing can take time. We don't automatically know the best way to shoot an arrow, climb a mountain, or lead an organization. We learn to do these things through slow learning processes where we try, fail, repeat.

To shift into a growth mindset, we have to change the way we learn. We have to be willing to learn slow and grow slow. We take each incremental step to growth. These small steps change *who* we are. After we take the step, we become someone new. We obtain new knowledge or new talents.

Eventually, we look back and can't believe the person we've become. It is no longer the weak, scared person we once were. Now, we're confident, strong, excited for the future. Learning slowly helps you in this process.

**TELL YOURSELF A DIFFERENT STORY:**

We are where we are through the stories we tell ourselves. We put on a soundtrack that tells us we're never going to amount to anything or that our latest failure will be the death of us. Neither of these things are true, but we tell them to ourselves anyway.

The negative stories we tell are damaging. They hurt our self-esteem. They stop our growth. We have to tell ourselves a different story.

Think of George Bailey in *It's a Wonderful Life*. George had a negative soundtrack playing in his head. He told himself that the world would be a better place had he never existed, and he was ready to commit suicide by jumping off a bridge. He pressed play on the negative soundtrack.

However, in the movie, Clarence, an angel, comes and helps George realize he is wrong.

Clarence shows George the impact his life has had on the people around him by showing George a vision of the world without him. Mr. Gower goes to prison for manslaughter. His uncle Billy is institutionalized. The town George loved is full of unsavory people.

George learns the truth from the vision Clarence gave him. He is now able to tell himself a different story. He now has gratitude for the life he is still living.

What can you do to tell yourself a different story? How can you change the way you view your situation in life?

Write down the stories you're telling yourself. Listen to the words you've repeated in your head.

Once these stories are down on paper, review them. Ask yourself if the stories are really true. Many times, you will discover the stories are not reality. They're a distorted sense of who you are. By working through your thoughts, you begin to see what you need to work on.

When you do, you will learn things are better than they appear. It will give you a new zest for your leadership position. You will be able to help the people you've longed to help.

## DISCUSSION QUESTIONS:

1. We all have weaknesses. Are you embracing your weakness or hiding from it?
2. Learning can happen quickly or slowly. Do you have a time when you slowed down your learning to enhance the experience? What did you learn from this slowing down?
3. Our stories define us. The stories we tell can trap us in a Groundhog Day loop or it can break us free. What story do you need to change in your life?

## SCENE 13:

# KEEPING COMMITMENTS

———

*"I want to build something. Make things grow. That takes hard work. A lifetime of it. That's not why a man comes to a pretty woman. After a while I won't be so pretty. But this land will be."*

—HANNAH, *SILVERADO*

What does commitment look like? How does commitment impact the way you lead? Does the commitment your team has to you and the organization matter?

Brent Baum was part of the startup team at DreamWorks. He worked on the ten-year business plans for all the different divisions at the studio. He worked on blockbuster movies, such as the animated movie *Finding Nemo*. He also earned a Wharton MBA and a masters in Asian studies from the University of Pennsylvania.

In my interview with Baum, he shared details about his time working on the *Finding Noah* documentary.

*Finding Noah* is a documentary about the search for Noah's Ark, but we're not here to debate whether Noah's Ark is historical or fictional.

It also wasn't Baum's intent to debate it. What he wanted to do while filming the documentary was see if they could find the ark that has been talked about so much.

My interview with Baum took an interesting turn when we got to the *Finding Noah* story. My friend Kevin DeVries worked with Baum on this project. DeVries was one of the explorers looking for the ark. Baum was one of the film crew. They're two distinct parties in the movie, but they both overlap in a fascinating story.

This story takes place when the crew was in Turkey.

There's a political group in Turkey designated as a terrorist organization by the United States government. The group is the Kurdistan Workers Party, or PKK for short. They've been fighting for Kurdish independence from the Turkish government for years.

Before heading to Mount Ararat to film the exploration, Baum had to go to the Kurdish tribal leaders and work with them. This meant getting Kurdish vehicles, Kurdish horses, and supplies from the Kurdish people. They got approval from the village elders, and everything seemed fine.

One day, a young boy runs into the Kurdish camp carrying a note. He hands it to the Kurdish leaders, and a buzz runs through the village. According to Baum, the people are frantic. They're looking at Baum and calling him the White Kurd. The leader of the Kurds came over to Baum and placed his hand on Baum's shoulder. The leader then tells Baum they're in big, big trouble. The PKK wants to meet and they want $500,000, or they're not going to get off the mountain.

Baum calls the two groups together, the excavation team and the film team. These teams had been two fairly separate groups, but they had come together as Baum proved himself to the excavation team. He let the two groups know what was going on. He told them he could only take one person to meet with the PKK forces. When he asked who was willing to go, everyone raised their hand and said they were going to go.

This was all through the building of trust.

Then, he gave everyone an option. He told everyone working on the *Finding Noah* documentary that he couldn't keep any of them there. He wasn't going to force them to stay. They could leave if they so desired. One of the people was Baum's business partner and longtime friend. His friend chose to take the option to get out of Dodge. His friend said he has two kids. He wanted to leave. Baum tells him to go.

The choice Baum's friend made hurt Baum deeply. It was a shattering of trust—one he and his friend had spent years building. Baum understood his friend's desire to leave. The man had a wife and kids. He wanted to see them again. However, Baum pointed out that they had made a commitment to the film, the crew, and the people around him.

In our interview, Baum told me what he told his friend. The words weren't cold. They were caring but tough. These were the words he spoke to his now former friend.

"So did that guy on the top of the mountain, and so does that guy at 4,200-meter camp. Not just one guy but a bunch of the guys on our team that are up there, and this kid right here who volunteered to come with me to go talk to the PKK has a newborn. His wife gave birth right before we came on this trip. Right, and his brother is up there, and he has young kids. And these kids from Montana and Washington and Utah, Texas, who I got on my crew because I couldn't take normal Hollywood camera radios out there."

Everyone on the team had made a commitment to the film. They had committed to the director, Baum. More importantly, they had all committed to each other to see the project through. They had to come to rely on that commitment with each other. Without it, they would be lost.

Baum continued, "Those Hollywood guys couldn't survive in that environment. So, they all say they're going to stay, and I say to the people who wanted to leave, 'Well you need to get out of here.' I can't leave. Because I told that guy's wife that he would be okay. There are a dozen of them that I said that to their wife. Now, when you're put in an extreme situation, you start to redefine the boundaries of leadership."

Baum felt he couldn't leave. He didn't have a choice to back out of his commitment. He had given his word to the many people on his crew that he would stand with them during this journey. More than that, Baum had made a commitment to the families of the men and women he was leading on this documentary filming.

He wanted his word to mean something. He chose to keep his commitment regardless of the danger to himself.

He wanted his word to mean something. He chose to keep his commitment regardless of the danger to himself.

## WHY COMMITMENTS MATTER

I've experienced far too many leaders who feel that the people they lead need to keep their commitments. If a member of their team says they're going to do it, by golly, they better make sure it gets done. I understand their desire for people to keep their commitments. It's one of the tenets of trust.

However, these same leaders struggle with keeping *their* commitments. They believe, falsely, that because of their position in an organization, they can make and break commitments without consequence. These leaders are wrong. The constant making and breaking of commitments wears on those they lead. Their team begins to feel maligned and abused. They don't know if they can believe what the leader is saying.

I experienced a leader breaking their commitments early on in my career. It was a frustrating experience, and one that bothered me to no end. Because the leader of the organization would say one thing and do another, I never knew what I should be doing. I also felt as if I could never trust the leader of the organization. It was one failed promise after another.

The leader lacked the ability to commit to the words he had said. My time at the organization was more miserable than enjoyable. With the leader unable to keep his commitments, many of the team members failed to keep their commitments as well. Talk about a bad workplace.

While the ability to keep commitments extols the leader's integrity, keeping commitments goes beyond that. Commitment matters for three reasons.

### 1. YOUR TEAM KNOWS WHAT TO EXPECT:

There are movie franchises that you know what you can expect. *The Fast and the Furious* movie franchise is one of these series. You know going into the theater you're not going to get a Golden Globe-winning movie. Rather, you go in expecting to see fast cars, outlandish situations, and a movie about family.

Imagine going into a workplace and not knowing what to expect. You may have a project you've poured hours into suddenly scrubbed from the board tracking progress. Maybe you see someone being handed their pink slip after faithfully following the organization's leader, only to have the leader turn around and stab them in the back.

This doesn't happen by mistake. This happens when leaders cannot stay committed. They constantly change the bar of what a person must do. They raise or lower the bar on a whim, all based on how they're feeling that morning. It's a hard environment to work in.

You don't want this for yourself. You need to make sure you're not giving this to the teams you lead.

To help with this, you need to make sure you're fully committed to the organization and the team. You do this by backing up their projects. You help them know what is important and what needs to be worked on. You stop changing course every other day. You stay the course with your people.

### 2. YOUR COMMUNICATION IS CLEARER:

In the 2016 movie *Arrival*, Dr. Louise Banks approaches language as a mathematician. Scientists are trying to communicate with aliens. The aliens are asked simple questions. Their responses are symbols that the scientists cannot understand. The communication between the two parties is not clear until Dr. Banks is able to translate the symbols.

Something happens when you don't keep your commitments. Not only do your team members and customers not know what to expect, but they also see your communication lacking clarity. This is because a lack of commitment kills clarity.

You have to stop and think about what you had committed to. You then have to figure out whether or not you followed through on the commitment. Last, but not least, you may backtrack because of a commitment that was broken.

Each of these things breaks down the clarity of your communication. You can't be clear if you're constantly changing directions, goals, and commitments. Make sure you're following through on your commitments so you can clearly communicate.

### 3. YOU ARE SEEN AS TRUSTWORTHY:

Alfred Pennyworth is Bruce Wayne's butler in *The Dark Knight*. Pennyworth is steady, loyal, and trustworthy. Bruce Wayne trusts Pennyworth with his secret identity and, more importantly, his life. Pennyworth is there to bandage wounds, cook meals, and be a friend. I'm not sure we could find a more trustworthy example in film than Alfred Pennyworth.

More than anything, a failure to follow through on your commitments tells those you're leading that you are not a trustworthy individual.

This is what happened with the leader I mentioned earlier. His lack of keeping his commitments changed the way I saw him. I saw him as someone who I couldn't trust because I knew he wouldn't follow through on what he said.

We don't want to be seen as untrustworthy; we want to be seen as a trusted source. We want people to have the confidence that we're going to do what we say we're going to do. We can't do that if we don't keep our commitments.

## KEEPING COMMITMENTS ISN'T EASY

With all of this, you may think that keeping your commitments will be easy. Everyone wants their team to know what to expect, to communicate clearly, and to be seen as trustworthy. Who wouldn't keep their commitments knowing this?

Almost everyone.

We've all broken our commitments. We've told our wives that we would take out the trash. Trash day comes and goes, and the garbage can sits next to the house instead of on the terrace.

Or you told Mary in accounting that you would have the details of a financial transaction to her. Guess what's missing? The details you promised.

It's amazing that commitments are so hard to keep. That tells us a lot about ourselves.

It also tells us that there is a huge gap in our integrity when we can't keep our commitments. That means we all have a big opportunity to improve in this area. That's a good thing. That means we can improve.

Let's all make the commitment today to become better at keeping commitments.

## DISCUSSION QUESTIONS:

1. Does your team know what to expect from you and your organization? How can you better inform your team of what they can expect?
2. How can you communicate more clearly? Are there areas you're struggling to communicate?
3. Where do you struggle with being trustworthy? What actions need to change so your team can trust you?
4. Think about a commitment you broke. Why did you break it? What could you do to make it right?

# ACT 3

# SCENE 14:

# WHAT NOW?

———

*"To infinity and beyond!"*

—BUZZ LIGHTYEAR, *TOY STORY*

We've journeyed through the history of film. We've taken a look at the history of leadership, and we've looked at leadership in the movies. It's been a fascinating journey, but it doesn't stop there. I want to share a couple more things with you.

What I'm about to share with you will help *you* connect the films you watch to the way you lead. It will help cement the fact that screen time isn't bad time. The time you spend in front of a movie theater screen or a television screen can actually benefit you.

We can rejoice in this. We can be excited. We also need to make sure we're aware of why we're watching films. The reason for watching films can be multifaceted. Personally, I watch films because:

### I ENJOY THE GREAT STORIES TOLD

On average, it takes 588 people to make a movie. Working with so many cast members can be daunting. Yet, so many directors can still get a great story out to the audience.

Writers and directors craft vivid stories that help audiences step into another world. We hear the ideas that have been rattling around in the minds of movie producers and story writers. This gives us the ability to step into their worlds and experience our lives from a different perspective.

### I ENJOY THE EXPERIENCE OF A THEATER

There's something special about walking into a theater. The smell of the fresh popcorn popping. The hustle and bustle of the crowds of people also seeing the movie with me. The comfortable recliners. The experience I get to share with other moviegoers. Last, but definitely not least, I enjoy the time I get to spend with my bride watching the films together.

### I ENJOY THE SHARING OF WISDOM

Movies are more than just the flashing pictures on the screen. It's more than the dialogue shared by the cast members. It's more than the experience shared between moviegoers.

Watching a movie shares wisdom. Wisdom is shared through the stories that are told.
- We can see why the villain may have betrayed the beloved hero. This helps us to understand why good people go bad.
- We saw this in *Spider-Man 3* as Harry Osborne betrayed Peter Parker.

- We see how a simple solution can solve a large problem.
- In the movie *Signs*, the solution to the alien invasion was that water could kill the aliens.
- Or, we see a down-and-out salesman overcome his troubled past by working hard and smart to become a great success.
- Success meant becoming a Wall Street stock trader in the movie *The Pursuit of Happyness*.

We only have to open our eyes. When we do, we can see film as more than we once thought.

In the next few chapters, we're going to look at ways to learn from the big screen. I am going to share how I have been able to watch a movie and pick out the leadership lessons being shown on the screen. I want these next few chapters to help *you* become a *reel leader*. It is possible. You can do it.

## DISCUSSION QUESTIONS:

1. What do you most enjoy about the movie experience? Why is this?
2. How does learning from the movies benefit from the shared experience?
3. What is your favorite memory from a movie experience?
4. What's the next movie you're going to watch? How are you going to view it differently?

# SCENE 15:

# HOW TO FIND LEADERSHIP LESSONS IN FILM

———

*"To find something, anything, a great truth or a lost pair of glasses, you must first believe there would be some advantage in finding it. I found something a long time ago and have held on to it for grim death ever since. I owe my success in life to it; it put me where I am today.*

—JACK BURDON, *ALL THE KING'S MEN*

Finding leadership lessons in film may not come as easily to you as it does to me now. Then again, looking for leadership lessons didn't come naturally to me. I had to hone my skills and *really* begin looking at film in another way.

Building the skill took time. Building the skill was a lot like building a muscle. You don't do it once and become ripped like Arnold Schwarzenegger in *The Terminator*. No, it takes hard work and intentionality.

Brian Dodd is the executive director of new ministry partnerships for INJOY Stewardship Solutions. In this role, he does leadership development, capital campaigns, developing a pathway to have cultures of generosity, and more for churches. However, at night, he throws on a different hat. Brian throws on the hat of leadership blogger at his website, *Brian Dodd on Leadership*. This is where he really flexes his leadership knowledge.

Brian is a lot like me. He enjoys film and movies. He loves to go to his local Cineplex and catch the latest movie playing. He also loves to write about movies and how they can be used to teach leadership. The way he does this is engaging.

In talking with Brian, he shared a story about the way he uses movies to teach leadership. I believe his story will help you see a way to view movies with an eye toward leadership.

He talked openly about the way he looks at the films he watches. But what was most fascinating was when he described a leadership training program he ran with a group of business leaders. His method will help you see the leadership lessons in movies.

During the training program, Brian was teaching a group of local business leaders. His objective was to help these business leaders see leadership in everything that they see and do. He gave the business leaders an exercise. Brian showed these leaders a two-and-a-half-minute clip from the movie *Moneyball.*

*Moneyball* stars Brad Pitt as Billy Beane, the former general manager of the Oakland Athletics baseball team and how he transformed the game of baseball through the use of analytics.

The scene Brian showed was of Beane going into a parking garage with Jonah Hill's Peter Brand. Beane and Brand have a conversation about the medieval thinking in baseball. The prevailing thought had been that you bought wins. This wasn't what Beane and Brand thought. They believed you should buy runs.

After watching the clip, Brian asked the business leaders a simple question. He wanted them to tell him *every* leadership lesson they saw in the two-minute clip. The results were shocking. In the large room full of business leaders, the leaders could only name one single leadership lesson each.

Brian had seen ten or more lessons in the brief clip. He then walked the group through each lesson he saw, explaining where the lesson came from.

> Brian had seen ten or more lessons in the brief clip. He then walked the group through each lesson he saw, explaining where the lesson came from.

Next, Brian showed a clip from the film *Avengers: Endgame*. The scene shown was the final battle scene where Tony Stark has the Infinity Gauntlet. Tony snaps his fingers and turns Thanos and the other bad guys to dust. After showing this short clip to the business leaders, he asked the same question. He wanted to hear from them the leadership lessons they saw in the clip.

The response was much different this time. Instead of every leader having one answer, the business leaders began to spit out leadership lesson after leadership lesson. By the end of the clip, each business leader shared *at least* five lessons from the short clip.

The business leaders Brian taught began to see leadership lessons in film. They could look at a film or a short clip from a movie and extrapolate the leadership lessons displayed in the film. You can do the same thing.

## FINDING LEADERSHIP LESSONS

Finding the leadership lessons in movies isn't the most intuitive thing you do, at least not in the beginning. The more you work on this skill, the more leadership lessons you will begin to discover.

But how do you do this? You know you *can* find them, but you don't know *how*.

I remember the first time I began to look at movies with an eye toward leadership. I felt sloppy and unprepared. I didn't know what I was doing. I only knew that I *could* find lessons in film. So, I began to work on honing this skill. The film that rekindled it all was the 2014 remake of *RoboCop*.

When I looked back at the *Reel Leadership* article I had written for the film, I noticed I was a lot like those business leaders in Brian Dodd's training program. I couldn't pull out a lot of leadership lessons. In fact, I could only see five lessons in the film. These days, it is much different. Now, I find myself bringing a notebook to the theater. I write quotes and notes as I see them and then I transcribe what I have seen so I can remember them and share the leadership lessons with my blog audience.

But how do we evolve? How do we see the leadership lessons the movie is trying to teach us?

You can find leadership lessons in movies by doing the following:

### FIX YOUR MINDSET

The biggest thing you will have to do is to change your mindset when watching movies. You no longer go to the theater strictly to be entertained, though nothing is wrong with that. Instead, your mindset is one of growth and learning.

When you sit down in those comfy theater seats, your mind changes from "let's have fun" to "let's learn something today." It's a subtle shift that changes everything. It's for the better but sometimes you may get frustrated because your mindset automatically defaults to thinking about what happens in a movie through the lens of *Reel Leadership*.

Fixing your mindset will allow you to be ready to observe the movie through fresh eyes. Make sure your mindset is ready to learn.

**BE ON THE LOOKOUT**

You won't consciously take away leadership lessons from the movies you watch unless you're on the lookout.

Brian shared how he helped shift the focus of the business leaders. He helped open their eyes to all the leadership lessons swirling around in a movie.

You have to be on the lookout for leadership lessons. When you watch the movie, you will see a character do something. When the character takes a specific action, you must take notice.

Maybe it was the scene in *Unbroken* where Mac, Phil, and Zamperini are on a lifeboat, adrift in the ocean. Zamperini had set out a ration schedule for the chocolate bars they had. He knew they had to make their rations last as long as possible. Upon awakening the next morning, Phil and Zamperini discovered Mac had devoured all the chocolate. Nothing was left. The men had no food remaining.

In this scene, we can take away one major point. The selfish actions of one person can hurt those around them. When Mac ate the chocolate, he made the fear of the men dying from starvation a very real possibility.

Think about this in relation to the workplace. Selfishness creeps in. An employee or another leader sees that they can use company property for personal use without repercussions. They continue to use the property, failing to realize that each time they did it cost the organization money. Eventually, the fees for the piece of property they used add up, and they have to let someone go.

When you are on the lookout for a leadership lesson, you will discover a lesson. Be on the lookout!

**TALK ABOUT IT**

Movies are something we all talk about. We share our experiences and ideas about the movies we watch.

When I worked at Circuit City back in the early 2000s, I had a coworker who would regularly talk about movies. One of his favorite movies at the time was the new Ang Lee film, *Hulk*. The basis of this film was the Marvel comic book character, the Incredible Hulk.

My coworker and I discussed this movie so much. He loved the film. I cringed while watching it. Our opinions differed, but we could still discuss the movie and find common ground.

Had I been a *reel leader* back then, I would have been able to share my thoughts on the leadership lessons in the *Hulk* movie. Yet still today, I vividly remember the conversations Jerry and I had about it. He was so excited to see the big, green Hulk jumping and smashing that he couldn't contain his joy.

Sharing thoughts and opinions with Jerry about *Hulk* has stuck in my mind for twenty years.

When we talk about the movies we watch, we can dive deeper into the emotions, feelings, and ideas the movie made us feel and think about. We can flesh out the moral premise of the film. In doing so, we're able to remember the action-packed moments along with the leadership lessons we could see in the movie.

### TAKE NOTES

This idea may sound bonkers, but taking notes helps you realize the lessons a movie is trying to teach you. Every time I head to the theater, I bring one of my trusty notebooks. I've collected these throughout the years of conferences, running, etc. It doesn't really matter where I get the notebooks from; I use them to chronicle my thoughts during the movie-watching process.

By taking notes, you can write down the parts of the movie that truly speak to you. When you hear a line of dialogue that perks your ear, write it down. If there is an epic scene, note that moment in your notebook.

My notes are typically simple. They capture the idea of the scene or a quote. Here are a few examples from my notebook.

- "It is you that needs help." —Sensei
  - Haru notices a woman needs help. Tells sensei about woman. Sensei corrects him and tells him *he* needs help.
  - *Beverly Hills Ninja*

- Dell's wife is angry about the mistakes Dell had made. Wouldn't let him stay at her apartment. Dell kept putting family through the same junk.

  – *The Upside*
- Doc rescued by the Expendables team. Struggled to say thanks. Barney pressured Doc to say thanks. Show thankfulness.

  – *The Expendables 3*

Once the movie is over, flip through the notes you have taken. Review them. Maybe expand on them. Use your notebook to keep track of all the leadership lessons you see in the movie. You will discover the movie has spoken about leadership over and over again.

## DISCUSSION QUESTIONS:

1. How do you need to change the way you watch films so you can find the leadership lessons hidden within?
2. How do you remember quotes or scenes from movies? What do they mean to you?
3. Go watch a movie clip. Think of all the leadership lessons you saw. How many did you see?
4. Who can you help understand the value of movies?

## SCENE 16:

# THE REEL LEADERSHIP FRAMEWORK WITH TEAMS

———

*"No matter what anybody tells you, words and ideas can change the world."*

—JOHN KEATING, *DEAD POET'S SOCIETY*

We now know how to use *Reel Leadership* to make *ourselves* better leaders. We watch movies with intentionality.

The next question is how do we help those we lead become *reel leaders?* That's what this next chapter will help you discover.

I interviewed John Ramstead for the *Reel Leadership* podcast. John is a former Navy fighter pilot and was a part of the Top Gun Academy (like the Tom Cruise movie, but not). He is also a leadership coach and hosts the *Eternal Leadership* podcast.

John shared with me a story that took place when he was with a Fortune 100 company. The company took the management team on a retreat. There, they started the retreat by watching a movie called *Twelve O'Clock High*. The movie is a great black-and-white film starring Gregory Peck.

*Twelve O'Clock High* takes place in World War II. The focus is on a bomber command unit. Peck's character, General Savage, comes in and he's a hard-nosed, stern man. General Savage's hard-nosed leadership style works…for a time. Eventually, the brash leadership style stops working. General Savage recognizes this and has to change the way he leads.

John's boss used this example in film to help create a framework to understand teams of men and women in high-pressure situations. He had the team sit down and talk about what they saw. He created exercises for the team to walk through.

One such exercise went like this:
- The team watched a portion of the film.
- The team would talk about the film.
- Team members would have to role play how they would respond in a similar situation.
- Team members would have to give a reason for how they would respond.
- The team would finish watching the clip to see how the movie character responded.

This changed John's whole thinking about the way he could use and view movies. He now had a framework to help him examine movies. Movies were no longer mindless entertainment for him.

We see a shift in how we view movies when we realize there are different ways to watch movies. We can all build our own unique framework for becoming a *reel leader*. However, I believe the framework I have come up with and the framework John had seen in use are perfect tools anyone can use to extract valuable leadership insights from movies and help their teams to use as well.

## We see a shift in how we view movies when we realize there are different ways to watch movies.

The rest of this chapter looks at an example of this framework using Ramstead's exercise. We will see how to look at movies in a new way, what steps you need to take, what steps your team members need to take, and how this framework all comes together to help us make better use of our time watching what even John Ramstead once considered mindless entertainment.

### THE *REEL LEADERSHIP* FRAMEWORK

This section of the chapter is all about the framework for *Reel Leadership*. We're going to dive into the five-step process of gaining leadership insights from the movies. This *Reel Leadership* framework will change the way your team views movies for the rest of their lives.

**WATCH A MOVIE CLIP:**

You can't extract knowledge from movies without a movie clip! You're going to have to watch a few of your favorite movies again... Oh, the horror! Right?

- What's happening?
- Who's doing the right thing?
- Who's going against the grain?
- What are the results?

You will need to figure out what you've just watched. The above questions will help with that, and you should now have an idea of what *you* would do in the same situation if you were in the movie.

Now, it's time to introduce the movie clip to your team.

**1. HAVE YOUR TEAM WATCH THE MOVIE CLIP YOU WATCHED:**

Introduce the movie clip to your team. Show them a thirty-second to five-minute movie clip. Whether you choose to show them a movie clip from *The Fast and the Furious*, *Wonder Woman*, *Jaws*, *Back to the Future*, *Forrest Gump*, or *Ghostbusters*, your team will respond with enthusiasm. They get to have fun while learning.

For example, there's a terrific scene in *Wonder Woman* called "No Man's Land." In it, Gal Gadot's Diana (Wonder Woman's civilian identity) is walking through a war zone with Steve Trevor. Diana hears the call of a woman needing help. She stops to offer what aid she can. Then she continues with Steve to the other soldiers. They're hesitant to step onto the battlefield. Diana isn't. She puts on her crown, steps across the barricade, and engages the enemy.

Before you start the clip, it's probably a good idea to explain the reason behind watching it. Help your team understand the value of watching a "mindless" piece of entertainment by telling them what you're going to do next. This is where the real fun begins.

### 2. HAVE YOUR TEAM TALK ABOUT THE MOVIE CLIP:

You're now going to ask your team to huddle together in small groups to discuss what they saw in the movie clip.

Did they see someone exhibiting positive leadership traits? Was the leader a negative leader? How is the choice the character made going to impact those around them?

Get your team talking. They're going to love this because they get to insert their opinion on what they just watched. They're also going to hear from others in the room. This helps them hear varying viewpoints and ideas about what could happen. This stretches their ideas and introduces them to new ideas they may not have thought about.

At a recent Comic Con presentation, I shared the clip I mentioned above from *Wonder Woman*. After showing the clip, I asked the audience multiple questions. I created a conversation around the scene, and the audience began buzzing with chatter. The ideas they exchanged started off short. There were also few answers until others started answering.

Talking about the scene engaged the audience. It got them thinking about leadership in the movie.

### 3. HAVE YOUR TEAM ROLE-PLAY THEIR RESPONSE:
Now, your team needs to show *how* they would respond.

In their small groups, have each team member play out their response to the situation that happened in the movie clip. Have them walk through their feelings and why they're responding the way they are. This will help them process their thoughts in a tangible way.

Involve as many people as you can in this exercise. You will want multiple people working in tandem to make this a great experience. Let them play out their ideas to the end. Have them create their own ideas of what will happen if the characters continue down path A, B, or C.

You will see your team be extremely creative in the situations they dream up. They will play out the scenarios in ways you never would have thought of. They will also see how different reactions to the scenarios will change the end result.

At the same Comic Con, I asked the audience members what they would have done. They walked me through their responses. They shared their actions and what would happen after making the choice. It was eye-opening for them!

**4. HAVE YOUR TEAM EXPLAIN THEIR CHOICES:**

Everyone has a reason for the way they respond. You won't think the same way as I do. I won't think the same way you do. Bob in accounting will think completely differently than you or me. That's what makes this piece of the framework so interesting.

We get to hear the reasoning behind people's actions. We get to see inside of their thinking patterns.

As your team explains their choices, you will see they did not make their decisions without thought. Each person who responds will have a thoughtful answer. Some of these answers will make you challenge your own assumptions. They will make their team members challenge their assumptions.

These same Comic Con attendees then shared their reasoning for their choices. Each person had a great answer for the reasoning behind their decision. One audience member shared how he wanted to be tactical with his decisions. Another shared how he would have felt comfortable going forward because of the abilities of Wonder Woman. Everyone had a different reason, but all the reasons were valid.

Now, it's time to move onto the final step of the *Reel Leadership* framework.

## 5. WATCH THE REST OF THE MOVIE CLIP AND DISCUSS THE OUTCOME:

Your team now has an idea of how they would respond. Now it is time to see how the actors, director, and producer had the characters respond.

Keep an eye on each character in the scene. They will all have a reaction. One may be the antagonist. Another will be the hero. Still another may be the innocent bystander. Everyone has a role to play in the outcome.

Once the scene completes, have your team members gather around to discuss what happened. They will share their ideas, and you will share your ideas. Talk about everything that happened, including the characters and their reactions.

Have your team discuss why they think the characters made the choices they made. Have them also discuss how the choices of individuals in the movie clip impact other characters.

Last but not least, we finished watching the movie clip at Comic Con. After the clip played, we finished discussing the scene. Some of the audience members changed what they would have done. Others stuck to their guns. The discussion continued and grew deeper. It was a learning experience for everyone there.

This framework can take thirty-minutes to an hour, easily. It might even go longer than this if the discussion gets really good. *And it will.* Be ready to keep the conversation open and going.

## DISCUSSION QUESTIONS:

1. Do you have a framework for watching movies? What does the framework involve?
2. Are you comfortable using movies to teach your team? Why or why not?
3. How could movies become a critical part of your training programs?
4. What movie will you use to help your team understand leadership better?

# CREDITS

# CONCLUSION

———

*"Louis, I think this is the beginning of a beautiful friendship."*
—RICK BLAINE, *CASABLANCA*

Whoa! What a wild ride this has been, huh? We've examined the crazy world of film. The way film has evolved since its creation is insane. From the short clips considered groundbreaking to the latest and greatest blockbusters, the world of film has changed.

We also explored the history of leadership. We looked at a few examples of bad leadership, good leadership, and what it meant for the world. Leadership is still around today. In fact, I believe it is more important than ever with the way businesses are run. Without effective leadership, we're bound to be lost.

The next thing we explored was leadership *IN* film. Who would have thought there were so many valuable leadership lessons we could find in the films we watch from our couch or in the movie theater?

Leadership experts such as David Kahn, John Ramstead, Kary Oberbrunner, and others clued us into the leadership lessons they have discovered in the films they've watched. They explained how film transformed their lives.

Not only that, but you got a peek inside the minds of those creating the films we watch. David Hayter helped us understand we may have to use a more aggressive style of leadership at times. Brent Baum helped us see that keeping your commitments is important, even when times are tough. And Daniel Knudsen introduced us to the moral premise and how every great film has a moral premise (or great leadership lesson!).

## The *Reel Leadership* framework will help you understand and process movies in a way you have never dreamed of.

You now have a framework to view and teach movies in a different way. You can begin implementing the *Reel Leadership* framework with your teams today. Use the framework I shared in the previous chapter to help your team watch movies in a new way and to see leadership lessons in those movies. This will help your team grow and your organization become better.

As the lights dim and the curtain closes on this *Reel Leadership* book, I hope you realize screen time isn't bad. We can watch a film with an eye toward learning and growth. We can walk away from what many people would call a mindless activity, but we walk away with a slew of new insights into leadership. We have flipped the switch from a mindless consumer to that of a *reel* leader. We no longer watch movies for the entertainment value alone, though something is to be said for purely enjoying a movie for its artistic and cinematic value. We now watch movies to learn and grow and become our better selves.

I hope the window we've opened with *Reel Leadership* won't close as you close the pages of this book.

Rather, now that the window is open, why not make it permanent and use a prop stick so it will not close on you. You've now got your eyes open for everything a movie offers.

The end? Or, until there is a sequel....

# ACKNOWLEDGMENTS

―――――

*"The world will break your heart ten ways to Sunday. That's guaranteed. I can't begin to explain that. Or the craziness inside myself and everyone else. But guess what? Sunday's my favorite day again. I think of what everyone did for me, and I feel like a very lucky guy."*

―PAT SOLITANO, JR., *SILVER LININGS PLAYBOOK*

*Reel Leadership* was a labor of love. It also was a time commitment. Writing this book took me away from my wife, Pamela, for a period of time. Thank you for letting me pursue this book, write my words, and release it to the world. I love and cherish you more than words can express.

I wouldn't have been able to write this book without the knowledge and wisdom of many people. It was a privilege to interview the great actors, movie producers, and leaders mentioned in this book. Their insights made this book much better than it should have been. I learned so much from all of you.

David Hayter
Daniel Knudsen
Patrick Lencioni
Jon D. Harrison
Skip Prichard
John Ramstead

Brent Baum
Stanley D. Williams
Marty Himmel
Kary Oberbrunner
David Kahn
Brian Dodd

I would also like to thank those who supported the book through the Indiegogo crowdfunding campaign. Without your support, this book would not have happened.

Aaron Sorrels
Adam and Tracy Carafelle
Amanda White
Andy Near
Ashley Irvine
Pastor Ben and Jessica Vegh
Bill and Renee Embil
Bob Fitzgerald
Brandon Gerard
Brian Fletcher
Bruce and Brittany Harrier
Casey Bailey
Cassius Rhue

Chad Sayen
Chase Eskelsen
Craig Youn
Dan Vaughan
Darren Anderson
David Gray

Adam and Brittany Aldridge
Adam Smith
Amber Seewald
Annemarie Spadafore
Barb Sheren
Beth Beutler
Billy Baclom
Bobbi Crampton
Brandon Posivak
Brian Victor Streeter
Carol Peterson
Cassidy Knebl
Celeste Kieft
(and the Bold Furniture team)
Charles Singh
Chester W. Goad
Curtis Weibel
Daniel Hefferan
Dave Medendorp
David J. Nemes

David and Sarah Neubauer
Diana Breternitz
Eric Jacobson
Eric Anderson
Glenn and Morgan Paddock
Jonathan Harrison
Hilary Jastram
Janet Miles
Jason Koert
Jeff Rolff
Jennifer and James Zuidema
(and James, Jude, and Jiovanni)
Jeremy Babcock
Jimmi and Erica Costello
Jinny Uppal
Joe Simila
John Orton
Jordan Ring
Karen Sattory
Kevin Devries
Kevin Watson
Laura Seymour
Liam Seewald
Liah LaVassuer
Marco Riolo
Mark Nation
Mark Wiggin
Matthias Kuehnelt
Michael Acton
Michelle Stoner
Mike Spring
Nathan Magnuson

Dee Ann Turner
Douglas Hill
Eric Koester
Gary R. Hassenstab
Greg and Mandy Childrehose
Heather and Stacy Star
Jacob Scott
Jared Easley
Jeff and Lisa Eikenberry
Jeff Rush
Jen Way
Jerrod Mason
Jimmy Burgess
Jonaite Thomas
John Gradin
John Ramstead
Karen Johnson
Kenneth Overman
Kevin Lee
Kyle and Bobby Hill
Lawrence D. Lewis
Leo J. Lampinen
Linda Hoenigsberg
Marietta Lalonde
Mark Olsen
Marty Himmel
Melissa Medendorp
Michael Bungay Stanier
Mike Beall
Monica Sterns
Nick and Malinda Page

Nikki Romani
Patrick McDaniel
Rich Avery
Richard Medcalf
Rob Rulison
Rob Sorbo
Ron Friedman
Sally Smith
Sandra Miles
Scott Teichmer
Spencer Vereecken
Steven Antioho
Tammy Wylie
Tom Harper
Tony Rehor
Zech Newman

Pamela Hoeft
Rachell Kitchen
Richard Lau
Rick Theule
Robert Smyser
Roger Knopf
Roz Henderson
Salvatore Constantino
Sara and Nate Plunkett
Sean Glombowski
Stan Phelps
Steven Nolasco
Tiffany VanderMolen
Tom Tate
William Stauter

A special thanks to Andy Near. His friendship and support to get this book published went above and beyond what I was expecting. His generosity also encouraged me to make bigger asks. Don't be afraid to ask for big things. You never know what you might receive! That's what you taught me, Andy! I hope this book will make you proud.

The writing of this book involved a lot more than I was expecting. My publisher, New Degree Press, and their team were a godsend. I want to say thank you to Professor Eric Koester, Founder of the Creator Institute. Thank you to my editors, Natalie Lucas and Sandy Huffman (you helped turn an ugly baby into a beautiful thing). Without you, I don't think this book would have happened.

# APPENDIX

———

**INTRODUCTION**

Avildsen, John G, dir. *Rocky*. 1976; Beverly Hills, CA: MGM, 2014. Blu-ray disc.

Columbus, Chris, dir. *Harry Potter and the Sorcerer's Stone*. 2001; Burbank, CA: Warner Brothers Pictures, 2016. Blu-ray disc.

Corley, Thomas C. *Rich Habits: The Daily Success Habits of Wealthy Individuals*. Langdon Street Press, 2010.

Green, Dave, dir. *Teenage Mutant Ninja Turtles 2: Out of the Shadows*. 2016; Hollywood, CA: Paramount Pictures, 2016. Blu-ray disc.

James, Steve, dir. *Life Itself*. 2014; New York City, NY: Magnolia Pictures, 2015. Blu-ray disc.

Maxwell, John C. "Your Influence Story." *The John Maxwell Leadership Podcast*. April 17, 2019. https://johnmaxwellleadershippodcast.com/episodes/john-maxwell-your-influence-inventory. Accessed May 6, 2021.

*Merriam-Webster*, s.v. "fable." Accessed October 4, 2021. https://www.merriam-webster.com/dictionary/fable.

Newell, Mike, dir. *Harry Potter and the Goblet of Fire*. 2005; Burbank, CA: Warner Brothers Pictures, 2016. Blu-ray disc.

Scorsese, Martin. dir. *The Departed*. 2006; Burbank, CA: Warner Brothers. 2007. Blu-ray disc.

Wachowski, Lana, Lilly Wachowski. dirs. *The Matrix*. 1999. Burbank, CA: Warner Brothers Pictures, 2010. Blu-ray disc.

Williams, Stanley D. *The Moral Premise: Harnessing Virtue & Vice for Box Office Success*. Michael Wiese Productions. 2006.

## SCENE 1

Advokat, Stephen. "New Era for Hollywood: VCR Profits Outstrip the Theaters." *Chicago Tribune*, Accessed August 30, 2021. https://www.chicagotribune.com/news/ct-xpm-1986-01-03-8601010445-story.html.

Britannica Beyond (website). Accessed May 6, 2021. https://beyond.britannica.com/how-much-was-charlie-chaplin-worth.

Burns, Scott Z. dir. *The Report*. Vice Studios. 2019.

Fox, Mark A. (June 1, 2018). "DRIVE-IN THEATRES, TECHNOLOGY, AND CULTURAL CHA." Gale Academic Onefile.

History of Information (website) Accessed May 3, 2021. https://www.historyofinformation.com/detail.php?id=3981.

Hollywood Lexicon. Star System. Accessed May 6, 2021. www.hollywoodlexicon.com/starsystem.html.

National Board of Review. Innovations in Cinema: AromaRama. Accessed April 19th, 2021. https://nationalboardofreview.org/2014/01/innovations-cinema-aromarama/.

Oldest.org Oldest Movies in The World. Accessed May 3, 2021. https://www.oldest.org/entertainment/movies/.

Patterson, John. "A History of 3D Cinema." *The Guardian,* Accessed April 19, 2021. https://www.theguardian.com/film/2009/aug/20/3d-film-history.

**SCENE 2**

Bacharach Leadership Group. 4 Mistakes Made by History's Biggest Leaders. Accessed April 25, 2021. https://blg-lead.com/4-mistakes-made-by-historys-biggest-leaders/.

Carlin, David. "World War II: How Western Leaders Failed to Stop the Nazi Rise." *Forbes,* Accessed April 25, 2021. https://www.forbes.com/sites/davidcarlin/2019/09/04/world-war-ii-how-western-leaders-failed-to-stop-the-nazi-rise/?sh=1351778124e7.

Fawcett, Bill. "10 of the Greatest Leadership Mistakes in History." *Huffington Post,* Accessed April 25, 2021. https://www.huffpost.com/entry/10-of-the-greatest-leader_b_2057685?slideshow=true#gallery/5e4efd6ee4b016168334153a/1.

Huston, John. dir. *The Maltese Falcon*. 1941; Burbank, CA: Warner Brothers Pictures, 2010. Blu-ray disc.

Inspiring Leadership Now. "10 of the Most Inspiring Leaders of All Time: Remarkable Stories of Iconic Trail Blazers Who Went from Adversity to Extraordinary & Redefined Leadership." Accessed April 25, 2021. https://www.inspiringleadershipnow. com/most-inspiring-leaders-redefine-leadership/.

John Maxwell Team, Accessed April 25, 2021. https://johnmax-wellteam.com/the-heart-of-leadership/.

Johnson, Craig. "Enron's Ethical Collapse: Lessons for Leadership Educators." *Journal of Leadership Education* 2, no. 1 (Summer2003). https://journalofleadershiped.org/wp-content/ uploads/2019/02/2_1_Johnson.pdf.

Leaders Excellence Harvard Square. "The Evolution of Leadership." Accessed April 25, 2021. https://leadersexcellence.com/ the-evolution-of-leadership/.

*Merriam-Webster*, s.v. "leadership." Accessed May 3, 2021. https:// www.merriam-webster.com/dictionary/leadership.

Virginia Tech College of Liberal Arts and Human Sciences. "History Repeating." *illumiNation* 1 (2016-2017). Accessed April 25, 2021. https://liberalarts.vt.edu/magazine/2017/history-re-peating.html.

## SCENE 3

iEduNote. "5 Principles of Learning." Accessed May 3rd, 2021. https://www.iedunote.com/principles-of-learning.

Learn Through Experience. Learning Through Your Senses. Accessed May 3rd, 2021. https://learnthroughexperience.org/.

McQuoid, Simon. dir. *Mortal Kombat*. 2021; Burbank, CA: Warner Brothers Pictures. 2021, Blu-ray disc.

*Merriam-Webster*, s.v. "learn." Accessed May 3, 2021. https://www.merriam-webster.com/dictionary/learn.

Naishuller, Ilya, dir. *Nobody*. 2021; Los Angeles, CA: Universal Pictures Home Entertainment. 2021, Blu-ray disc.

Sakaguchi, Hironobu, Motonori Sakakibara. dirs. *Final Fantasty: The Spirits Within*. 2001; Culver City, CA: Sony Pictures Home Entertainment. 2007, Blu-ray disc.

## SCENE 4

John 15:12-14 (New Revised Standard Version).

Kershner, Irvin. dir. *Star Wars: Episode V - The Empire Strikes Back*. 1980; Los Angeles, CA: 20th Century Fox. 2016, Blu-ray disc.

Shelton, Ron. Dir. *Tin Cup*. 1996; Burbank, CA: Warner Brothers. 2020, Blu-ray disc.

## SCENE 5

Buck, Chris, Jennifer Lee. dirs. *Frozen*. 2013; Burbank, CA: Walt Disney Pictures. 2014. Blu-ray disc.

Gracey, Michael. dir. *The Greatest Showman*. 2017; Los Angeles, CA: 20th Century Fox. 2018, Blu-ray disc.

Shyamalan, M. Night. dir. *Signs*. 2002; Burbank, CA: Walt Disney Pictures. 2008. Blu-ray disc.

## SCENE 6

Bird, Brad, Jan Pinkava. dirs. *Ratatouille*. 2007; Burbank, CA: Walt Disney Pictures. 2019, Blu-ray disc.

Hancock, John Lee. dir. *The Little Things*. 2021; Burbank, CA: Warner Brothers. 2021, Blu-ray disc.

Lorenz, Robert. dir. *The Marksman*. 2021; Los Angeles, CA: Universal Pictures. 2021, Blu-ray disc.

McCracken, Brett. "Why We Watch Movies." *Relevant Magazine* (March 2010). Accessed September 1, 2021. https://www.relevantmagazine.com/culture/why-do-we-watch-movies/

Star Trek. Accessed September 7, 2021. https://www.startrek.com/database_article/tractor-beam

## SCENE 7

Cameron, James. dir. *The Terminator*. 1984; Burbank, CA: Warner Brothers. 2013, Blu-ray disc.

Lalonde, Joseph. "Meetings Must Die (How to Have More Productive Meetings)." *Joseph Lalonde*, January 12, 2018. https://www.jmlalonde.com/meetings-must-die-productive-meeting.

Lencioni, Patrick. "At the Table with Patrick Lencioni: Meetings and Movies." Produced by The Table Group. September 2019. (Accessed September 1, 2021). https://www.tablegroup.com/6-meetings-and-movies/.

Spielberg, Steven. dir. *Saving Private Ryan*. 1998; Hollywood, CA: Paramount Pictures. 2010, Blu-ray disc.

Zoom. About Us Page. https://explore.zoom.us/en/about/. Accessed May 14, 2021.

**SCENE 8**

Black, Rosemary. "Glossophobia (Fear of Public Speaking): Are You Glossophobic?" *Psychom*. Updated September 12, 2019. https://www.psycom.net/glossophobia-fear-of-public-speaking. Accessed May 21, 2021.

Craven, Wes. dir. *Scream*. 1996; Hollywood, CA: Paramount Pictures. 2021, Blu-ray disc.

Crowe, Cameron. dir. *We Bought a Zoo*. 2011; Los Angeles, CA: 20th Century Fox. 2012, Blu-ray disc.

Doane, Beth. "10 Female Leaders Share Their Biggest Fears and How They Overcame Them." *Darling Magazine*. https://blog.darlingmagazine.org/10-female-leaders-share-biggest-fears-overcame/. Accessed May 21st, 2021.

Gibson, Mel. dir. *Braveheart*. 1995; Burbank, CA: Warner Brothers. 2017, Blu-ray disc.

Heilpern, Will. "Richard Branson: I Am 'Naturally Shy' and 'I Still Get Nervous.'" *Business Insider*. August 10, 2016. Accessed May 21, 2021. https://www.businessinsider.in/richard-branson-i-am-naturally-shy-and-i-still-get-nervous/articleshow/53635422.cms?mobile=no.

Lee, Laura Walker's official website. "About." Accessed May 21, 2021. www.laurawalker.ventures/#about.

Pattison, Robert. "Robert Pattinson Uses Anxiety as a Charge on Set." *Sunday Today with Willie Geist,* November 27, 2019. https://www.today.com/video/robert-pattinson-uses-anxiety-as-a-charge-on-set-74172997592.

**SCENE 9**
Avildsen, John G. dir. *The Karate Kid*. 1984; Culver City, CA: Sony Pictures. 2010, Blu-ray disc.

*Merriam-Webster*, s.v. "self-mastery." Accessed September 2, 2021. https://www.merriam-webster.com/dictionary/self-mastery.

**SCENE 10**
Jackson, Peter. dir. *The Lord of the Rings Trilogy*. 2001, 2002, 2003; Burbank, CA: Warner Brothers. 2014, Blu-ray disc.

Pink, Daniel's website. "About." Accessed September 23, 2021. https://www.danpink.com/about/.

Ratner, Brett. dir. *X-Men: The Last Stand*. 2006; Los Angeles, CA: Twentieth Century Fox. 2011, Blu-ray disc.

Russo, Anthony, Joe Russo. dirs. *Captain America: Civil War*. 2016; Burbank, CA: Walt Disney Pictures. 2017, Blu-ray disc.

Watts, Jon. dir. *Spider-Man: Far from Home*. 2016; Culver City, CA: Sony Pictures. Marvel Studios. 2019.

## SCENE 11

Nayar, Vineet. "Three Differences Between Manages and Leaders." *Harvard Business Review*. August 2, 2013. Accessed September 24, 2021. https://hbr.org/2013/08/tests-of-a-leadership-transiti.

Singer, Bryan. dir. *X-Men: Days of Future Past*. 2014; Los Angeles, CA: Twentieth Century Fox. 2014, Blu-ray disc.

## SCENE 12

Capra, Frank. dir. *It's a Wonderful Life*. 1946; Hollywood, CA: Paramount Pictures. 2019, Blu-ray disc.

Dweck, Carol S. *Mindset: The New Psychology of Success Reprint, Updated Edition*, Kindle Edition. 2006.

Raimi, Sam. Dir. *Evil Dead II: Dead by Dawn*. 1987; Santa Monica, CA: Lionsgate Films. 2016, Blu-ray disc.

Rendall, David. *The Freak Factor: Discovering Uniqueness by Flaunting Weakness*. 2015.

Wachowski, Lana, Lilly Wachowski. Dir. *The Matrix*. 1999. Burbank, CA: Warner Brothers Pictures, 2010. Blu-ray disc.

## SCENE 13

Baum, Brent. dir. *Finding Noah*. 2015; Sun Valley, CA: Alchemy Studios. 2015, Blu-ray disc.

Cohen, Rob. dir. *The Fast and the Furious*. 2001; Los Angeles, CA: Universal Pictures Home Entertainment. 2017, Blu-ray disc.

Kasdan, Lawrence. dir. *Silverado*. 1985; Culver City, CA: Sony Pictures Home Entertainment. 2009, Blu-ray disc.

Willeneuve, Denis. dir. *Arrival*. 2016; Hollywood, CA: Paramount Pictures. 2017, Blu-ray disc.

## SCENE 14

Lasseter, John. dir. *Toy Story*. 1995; Burbank, CA: Walt Disney Pictures. 2010. DVD disc.

Muccino, Gabriele. dir. *The Pursuit of Happyness*. 2006; Culver City, CA: Sony Pictures Home Entertainment. 2007, Blu-ray disc.

Raimi, Sam. dir. *Spider-Man 3*. 2007; Culver City, CA: Sony Pictures Home Entertainment. 2012, Blu-ray disc.

Shyamalan, M. Night. dir. *Signs*. 2002; Burbank, CA: Walt Disney Pictures. 2008, Blu-ray disc.

## SCENE 15

Brian Dodd on Leadership. Website. https://brianddoddonleadership.com.

Burger, Neil. dir. *The Upside.* 2017; Los Angeles, CA: Universal Pictures Home Entertainment. 2019, Blu-ray disc.

Dugan, Dennis. dir. *Beverly Hills Ninja.* 1997; Culver City, CA: Tri-Star Pictures. 1999, DVD disc.

Hughes, Patrick. dir. *The Expendables 3.* 2014; Santa Monica, CA: Lionsgate Films. 2014, Blu-ray disc.

Jolie, Angelina. dir. *Unbroken.* 2014; Los Angeles, CA: Universal Pictures Home Entertainment. 2015, Blu-ray disc.

Lalonde, Joseph. 5 "Leadership Lessons from The Robocop Remake." *Joseph Lalonde,* February 17, 2014. https://www.jmlalonde.com/5-leadership-lessons-robocop-remake/. Accessed September 10, 2021.

Miller, Bennett. dir. *Moneyball.* 2011; Culver City, CA: Sony Pictures Home Entertainment. 2012, Blu-ray disc.

Russo, Anthony, Joe Russo. dirs. *Avengers: Endgame.* 2019; Burbank, CA: Walt Disney Pictures. 2019. Blu-ray disc.

Zaillian, Steven. dir. *All the King's Men.* 2006; Culver City, CA: Sony Pictures Home Entertainment. 2006, Blu-ray disc.

## SCENE 16

Jenkins, Patty. dir. *Wonder Woman*. 2017; Burbank, CA: Warner Brothers Pictures, 2017. Blu-ray disc.

King, Henry. dir. *Twelve O'Clock High*. 1949; Los Angeles, CA: 20th Century Fox. 2011, Blu-ray disc.

Weir, Peter. dir. *Dead Poet's Society*. 1989; Burbank, CA: Walt Disney Pictures. 2012. Blu-ray disc.

## CONCLUSION

Curtiz, Michael. dir. *Casablanca*. 1942; Burbank, CA: Warner Brothers Pictures, 2018. Blu-ray disc.

## ACKNOWLEDGMENTS

Russell, David O. dir. *Silver Linings Playbook*. 2012; Santa Monica, CA: Lionsgate Films. 2014, Blu-ray disc.